The EASY
DASH DIET
COOKBOOK
FOR BEGINNERS

Overcome Hypertension and Lower Blood Pressure with a 1500-Day Supply of Delicious, Low-Sodium, and High-Potassium Recipes – Includes a 12-Week Meal Plan

ALLEGRA GOLDSTEIN

Dash Diet Cookbook for Beginners

ISBN: 979-8851522796

10 9 8 7 6 5 4 3 2 1

GET THE BONUSES NOW

TO DOWNLOAD THE DIGITAL VERSION OF THESE BONUSES
YOU DON'T NEED TO ENTER ANY DETAILS EXCEPT YOUR NAME AND EMAIL ADDRESS.

BONUS # 1

" Eating Out on the Dash Diet "

BONUS # 2

" Mindfulness and the DASH diet "

BONUS # 3

" The Ultimate DASH Diet Smoothie Guide "

SIMPLY SCAN THE QR CODE BELOW OR GO TO

http://bonusforbooks.com/allegra-goldstein-dd

TABLE OF
CONTENTS

5   Introduction

17   CHAPTER 1: Breakfast

24   CHAPTER 2: LunchThe

32   CHAPTER 3: Dinner

40   CHAPTER 4: Snacks and Appetizers

47   CHAPTER 5: Side Dishes

54   CHAPTER 6: Desserts

60   CHAPTER 7: Drinks

66   CHAPTER 8: Quick and Easy Meals

74   CHAPTER 9: Vegetarian/Vegan

82   CHAPTER 10: Special Occasions

91   12 – Weeks Meal Plan

       Index

       Conclusion

INTRODUCTION

HISTORY AND SCIENTIFIC BACKING OF THE DASH DIET   7

HEALTH BENEFITS OF THE DASH DIET   8

THE BASICS OF THE DASH DIET   10

WHAT TO EAT AND WHAT TO AVOID   11

   What to Eat: *11*

   What to Limit or Avoid: *12*

THE FLEXIBILITY AND ADAPTABILITY OF THE DASH DIET   12

THE ROLE OF PHYSICAL ACTIVITY   13

TRANSITIONING INTO RECIPES   14

Especially comparing to a diet low in total fat, the Dash diet has been shown to be over two times as efficient at lowering blood pressure levels. This is because the Dash diet stresses eating things that are high in potassium and low in salt. It follows the scientific principle of Load and Offset, which states that you should fill your plate with healthy foods such as whole grains, veggies, and lean proteins for six out of the seven days of the week, afterwards you should abstain from eating for one day.

This is going to assist you in maintaining a healthy metabolic rate whilst additionally assisting you in maintaining control of your blood pressure. The DASH study, which was conducted over the course of a number of years, provided the basis for the diet's fundamental tenets.

The National Heart, Lung, and Blood Institute came up with the Dash diet in order to diminish the risk of cardiovascular disease and high blood pressure. The American Heart Association states that 90% of Americans are unaware of their hypertensive condition. High blood pressure, often referred to as "the silent killer," lacks noticeable symptoms and is frequently undetected until it harms the cardiovascular system.

The aim of the Dash diet is to diminish the amount of salt (sodium) in food. Additionally, it suggests consuming foods which are rich in potassium, calcium, magnesium, and particular vitamins, including A, C, and E. Researchers think that hypertension is caused by the sodium in our diets, which raises our blood pressure and leads to the condition. Our blood pressure goes up in direct proportion to the amount of salt in our diet. As time passes, this can lead to a number of health problems, such as coronary artery disease and stroke.

The Dash diet is based on two principles:

1. A diet that is low in salt (or "balanced"), rich in fruits and vegetables, and that comprises a certain amount of foods high in lean protein (like meat, chicken, fish, and eggs), but that derives a maximum of thirty percent of its total daily calories from saturated fat.

2. physical activity to promote good cardiovascular health.

To maintain excellent health, the daily salt intake in a healthy diet should be no more than twenty-three hundred milligrams. The goal is to consume less sodium while getting in excess of just enough of the nutrients potassium, calcium, and magnesium through this eating plan.

The Dash diet is one that can assist in lowering blood pressure since it emphasizes decreasing the amount of sodium consumed while simultaneously elevating the consumption of potassium, phosphorus, and magnesium. People can lower their systolic blood pressure by an average of five mm Hg and diastolic blood pressure by an average of two mm Hg if they adopt this diet for a minimum of two yrs. In addition, a recent study found that lowering sodium intake is associated with a greater reduction in systolic blood pressure than lowering saturated fat or total fat.

In addition to its positive effects on blood pressure, the Dash diet might also have potential benefits in enhancing sleep and mental well-being. Once opposed to a diet which included lower quantities of potassium and phosphorus, the Dash diet was shown to improve delta sleep ratings and general well-being of life in patients who suffered from hypertension, based on the findings of a review that analyzed clinical trials published in 2012 and conducted in the same year.

Initially, the Dash diet was suggested to patients who had previously taken drugs for high blood pressure; however, it can also be administered to healthy persons. It is currently one of the most well-liked diets available because of its ability to bring down high blood pressure.

The diet can be administered in a number of different ways. Since the Dash diet is typically connected with low-calorie diets, it is primarily utilized as a component of an overall strategy for weight reduction. Additionally, the Dash diet is followed by certain individuals in order to diminish their blood pressure (by itself), while others use it in order to lose weight, enhance their mental health, and increase the quality of sleep they get (a blend of all the factors mentioned).

History and Scientific Backing of the DASH Diet

The DASH diet, originating in the early 1990s, was developed following the groundbreaking DASH-Sodium trial. This trial, supported by the NHLBI in the US, contributed to the emergence of the DASH diet.

This dietary pattern aimed to combat high blood pressure and bolster heart health. Let's delve into the historical context and the scientific substantiation behind the DASH diet.

The DASH-Sodium trial, encompassing over 400 participants, randomized and meticulously investigated the effects of distinct diets on blood pressure, with a specific emphasis on sodium (salt) intake.

The primary objective was to identify an alternative, non-pharmacological approach to reducing elevated blood pressure, a critical risk factor for cardiovascular ailments.

The trial findings unequivocally demonstrated that the DASH diet, when coupled with a reduction in sodium intake, wielded significant efficacy in lowering blood pressure. In comparison to the control diet, the DASH diet produced a noteworthy average reduction of 5.5 mm Hg in systolic blood pressure (the upper number) and 3 mm Hg in diastolic blood pressure (the lower number). These outcomes remained consistent for individuals with hypertension as well as those with normal blood pressure. Subsequent to the seminal DASH-Sodium trial, numerous studies have consistently affirmed the health benefits associated with the DASH diet. Here are the key scientific discoveries:

1. Blood Pressure Reduction: Multiple studies have conclusively demonstrated the ability of the DASH diet to effectively lower blood pressure in individuals with hypertension as well as those with normal blood pressure.

2. Cardiovascular Health: Adhering to the DASH diet has been related to a reduced risk of cardiovascular diseases, encompassing heart disease, heart failure, and stroke.

3. Cholesterol and Lipid Profile: The DASH diet has been proven to enhance lipid profiles by diminishing total cholesterol, LDL cholesterol (commonly known as the "bad" cholesterol), and triglyceride levels.

4. Diabetes Management: Research suggests that the DASH diet can be advantageous for individuals with type 2 diabetes by improving glycemic control and insulin sensitivity.

5. Weight Management: The DASH diet actively supports healthy weight management, primarily due to its emphasis on fruits, vegetables, whole grains, lean proteins, and reduced saturated fat and added sugars. It has exhibited potential for both weight loss and weight maintenance.

6. Overall Health Benefits: The DASH diet promotes a well-balanced approach to nutrition, ensuring adequate nutrient intake, antioxidant provision, and fiber consumption. It aligns harmoniously with general guidelines for healthy eating and yields improvements in overall health and well-being.

Health Benefits of the DASH Diet

Reduces Obesity

A diet that is both well-balanced and healthy will continue to have two known effects on the body. The first of these is that it revs up the metabolism to a high pace, that in turn breaks down every one of the fatty deposits that have been deposited in the body. As a result, the DASH diet, which is high in fiber and low in fat, can assist with weight loss if it is adhered to religiously and with an emphasis on maintaining a healthy check and balance. In addition to that, you have to work out.

Fighting Against Osteoporosis

Because it is rich in potassium, calcium, and proteins, the DASH diet helps to avoid osteoporosis, which is characterized by a loss of bone density and structural integrity. However, this disease has a high prevalence rate among women who are at least that much older than middle age. When following this meal plan and maintaining a consistent consumption, the calcium to potassium ratio is maintained in a healthy range.

Improved Functioning Of The Kidney

With the assistance of potassium and sodium, kidneys are responsible for preserving the delicate fluid equilibrium that exists within the body. When this delicate equilibrium is thrown off, hypertension is the result. A high salt intake leads to increased retention of water in the body, which in turn leads to elevated blood pressure.

The fact that the DASH diet recommends maintaining a low salt consumption enables it to work like a miracle in combating this issue.

Because of the strain that it places on the kidneys as they attempt to rid the body of waste products and minerals in excessive amounts, high salt consumption has been related to kidney failure. Patients who are at an increased risk of kidney failure and who would like to minimize the incidence of kidney stones are encouraged to follow the DASH diet, since this eating plan has been promoted by the National Kidney Foundation. Mineral deposits can form along the inner lining of the kidneys, which can eventually lead to the formation of kidney stones.

Heart Disease

When you have a combination of high blood pressure, metabolic syndrome, and type 2 diabetes, you're likely to end up with heart disease. The fact that the DASH diet addresses all these conditions means that it can also eliminate your risk of heart disease. Even if you don't have any of these problems, this diet is still a great choice. Heart disease records the most significant number of deaths among Americans.

Metabolic Syndrome

Metabolic syndrome is a group of signs that can happen when you have too much insulin and are overweight. This syndrome is sometimes called "pre-diabetes" because it can lead to type 2 diabetes if it isn't taken care of.

Controlled Blood Pressure

It is the main benefit of the DASH diet and the reason why nutritionists and physicians recommend it. Following DASH lets you keep your blood pressure in check. This diet is ideal for anyone who is taking medication to control blood pressure and those with prehypertension symptoms and are looking for better ways of managing these symptoms. DASH is made to help bring down blood pressure and has been shown to work by science.

Healthy Cholesterol Levels

Since most of the fruits, beans, nuts, whole grains, and vegetables recommended under the DASH diet have high fiber content, you can eat them alongside fish and lean meat while limiting or regulating your intake of refined carbohydrates and sweets. It goes a long way in improving your cholesterol levels.

Decreased Risk Of Certain Cancers

Researchers have studied the relationship between the DASH diet and certain types of cancers and found a positive association that relates to reducing salt intake and monitoring dietary fat consumption. The diet is also low in red meat, which is linked to cancer of the rectum, colon, esophagus, lung, stomach, kidney, and prostate. Eating plenty of fresh produce helps prevent various types of cancer while emphasizing dairy products that are low in fat contributes to a drop in the risk of colon cancer.

Better Mental Health

The DASH diet will boost your mood while decreasing symptoms of mental health disorders like anxiety or depression. It is linked to making changes to your lifestyle, such as not smoking, drinking less booze, and working out daily. Moreover, the inclusion of nutrient-rich foods in the diet also helps balance hormones and chemicals in the brain and body, thus contributing to improved mental health and overall well-being.

Anti-Aging Properties

Many people who follow the DASH diet have attested to the fact that this diet helps to avoid some effects of aging so that they keep them feeling and looking younger. Increasing your consumption of fresh vegetables & fruits that are full of antioxidants will rejuvenate your hair and skin, revitalize and strengthen your joints, muscles, & bones, help you lose weight, and leave you feeling healthier.

The Basics of the DASH Diet

The DASH diet is a flexible & balanced eating plan intended to lower blood pressure & improve heart health. Here are the fundamental principles of the DASH diet:

1. Emphasis on Fruits and Vegetables: The DASH diet encourages the consumption of various fruits and vegetables, which are abundant in essential vitamins, minerals, and fiber. Aim to include multiple servings of fruits and vegetables in your daily meals and snacks.

2. Whole Grains: The DASH diet highlights the importance of whole grains such as brown rice, , oats, and quinoa. Compared to processed grains, these grains have more fiber and nutrients. Choose whole grain options for bread, cereals, pasta, and rice.

3. Lean Protein Sources: The DASH diet encourages eating lean meats, such as chicken, fish, beans, peas, and nuts. These protein sources are low in saturated fat and provide essential

nutrients such as omega-3 fatty acids and fiber. Limit the intake of high-fat meats and opt for healthier protein choices.

4. Low-Fat Dairy Products: The DASH diet inspires the consumption of low-fat or fat-free dairy products such as milk, yogurt, and cheese. Calcium and protein can be found in these dairy items. If you have lactose intolerance or prefer non-dairy options, there are alternatives like soy or almond milk fortified with calcium.

5. Limited Sodium Intake: Reducing sodium (salt) intake is a vital aspect of the DASH diet since excessive sodium consumption is associated with high blood pressure. Limit your intake of processed & packaged foods, which often contain high levels of sodium. Instead, opt for fresh foods and use herbs and spices to season your meals without relying on salt.

6. Moderate Consumption of Fats and Oils: The DASH diet recommends consuming healthy fats in moderation. Opt for sources like olive oil, canola oil, avocados, and nuts, which provide unsaturated fats. Eat less hot foods, fatty meats, and prepared snacks, which are high in saturated and trans fats.

7. Limited Added Sugars: The DASH diet discourages the consumption of added sugars. Cut down on how much sugary drinks, desserts, and prepared snacks you eat. Instead, eat naturally sweet foods like veggies when you want something sweet.

8. Portion Control: The DASH diet emphasizes the importance of portion control to maintain a healthy calorie balance. Pay attention to your portion sizes & listen to your body's cues of hunger and fullness. Ensure your meals include a variety of foods from different food groups.

9. Regular Physical Activity: While not exclusive to the DASH diet, incorporating regular physical activity is recommended for overall health and well-being. Engage in activities you relish, such as walking, swimming, cycling, or dancing, to complement your healthy eating habits.

What to Eat and What to Avoid

What to Eat:

1. Fruits: Include a variety of fresh or frozen fruits such as apples, bananas, oranges, berries, melons, and grapes. Aim for multiple servings per day.

2. Vegetables: Consume a wide range of vegetables, both raw and cooked. Include leafy greens, broccoli, carrots, tomatoes, peppers, and sweet potatoes. Try to have multiple servings each day.

3. Whole Grains: Choose whole grains like whole wheat, brown rice, oats, quinoa, whole grain bread, and whole grain pasta. Compared to processed carbs, these have a lot more fiber and nutrients.

4. Lean Proteins: Choose lean protein sources like skinless poultry, fish (such as salmon, trout, and tuna), legumes (beans and lentils), and tofu. Limit red meat consumption and opt for lean cuts when you do eat it.

5. Low-Fat Dairy: Include milk, yogurt, and cheese that are low in fat or have no fat at all. These give you calcium and protein without too much heavy fat. If you prefer non-dairy options, choose calcium-fortified alternatives like soy or almond milk.

6. Nuts, Seeds, and Legumes: Incorporate nuts (such as almonds, walnuts, and pistachios), seeds (flaxseeds, chia seeds), and legumes (chickpeas, black beans, lentils) for healthy fats, protein, and fiber.

7. Healthy Fats: Avocados, olive oil, canola oil, and nuts are all good sources of healthy fats. The monounsaturated and polyunsaturated fats in these foods are good for your heart health.

8. Herbs and Spices: Use herbs, spices, and sauces instead of too much salt to make your food taste better. Experiment with flavors like garlic, ginger, turmeric, cinnamon, and basil.

What to Limit or Avoid:

1. Sodium (Salt): Limit your intake of high-sodium foods such as processed & packaged foods, canned soups, condiments, and fast food. Aim to consume no more than 2,300 mg of sodium per day, or even less if you have high blood pressure.

2. Added Sugars: Minimize your consumption of added sugars found in sugary beverages, desserts, sweets, and processed snacks. Choose whole fruits to satisfy your sweet cravings.

3. Saturated and Trans Fats: Diminish your intake of saturated & trans fats found in fatty meats, full-fat dairy products, butter, fried foods, and commercially baked goods. Opt for lean protein sources & healthier fats.

4. Alcohol: Limit your alcohol consumption. Moderation is key, it is recommended to consult with your healthcare provider about the appropriate amount for you, as excessive alcohol intake can have negative health effects.

The Flexibility and Adaptability of the DASH Diet

One of the great advantages of the DASH diet is its flexibility and adaptability to various preferences and dietary needs. Here's how the DASH diet can be customized and adjusted:

1. Calorie Modification: The DASH diet can be adjusted to meet different calorie requirements. Whether you need to maintain your current weight, lose weight, or even gain weight, the DASH principles can be applied by adjusting portion sizes and calorie intake accordingly. Because of this, it can be used by people with different goals.

2. Personal Food Preferences: The DASH diet allows for personal food preferences and choices within its recommended food groups. You have the freedom to choose from a variety of fruits, vegetables, whole grains, lean proteins, and low-fat dairy products that you relish and that fit your taste preferences. This helps make the diet more sustainable in the long term.

3. Vegetarian or Vegan Adaptation: The DASH diet can be adapted to accommodate vegetarian or vegan lifestyles. Plant-based protein sources like legumes, tofu, tempeh, and seitan can replace meat and fish. Additionally, there are dairy-free alternatives available for those following a vegan approach.

4. Gluten-Free Considerations: For individuals with gluten intolerance or celiac disease, the DASH diet can be modified to be gluten-free. There are many gluten-free whole grains and alternative flours available that can be substituted for wtemp.-based products while still following the principles of the DASH diet.

5. Sodium Restriction: If you need to further restrict your sodium intake due to hypertension or other health concerns, the DASH diet can be adjusted accordingly. By focusing on fresh, whole foods and minimizing processed foods and added salt, you can diminish your sodium intake while still enjoying a nutritious diet.

6. Cultural and Ethnic Considerations: The DASH diet can be adapted to fit various cultural or ethnic cuisines. By incorporating traditional herbs, spices, and cooking techniques, you can infuse your cultural flavors into the DASH diet and maintain your cultural food identity.

7. Lifestyle Integration: The DASH diet can be seamlessly integrated into various lifestyles, including busy schedules, family meals, and dining out. Planning ahead, preparing meals in advance, and making informed choices when eating out can help you adhere to the DASH principles even in different situations.

The Role of Physical Activity

Physical activity plays a vital role in optimizing the effectiveness of the DASH (Dietary Approaches to Stop Hypertension) diet and promoting overall well-being through various means:

1. Blood Pressure Regulation: Engaging in aerobic exercises like brisk walking, jogging, cycling, or swimming for around 1fifty mins per week has proven effective in lowering both systolic & diastolic blood pressure levels, aligning with the primary goals of the DASH diet.

2. Cardiovascular Fitness: By blending the DASH diet with regular physical activity, cardiovascular health is further improved. Exercise strengthens the heart, enhances circulation, and helps maintain healthy cholesterol and triglyceride levels, ultimately reducing the risks of heart disease, heart failure, and stroke.

3. Weight Control: Physical activity plays a significant role in managing weight. When coupled with the balanced eating approach of the DASH diet, regular exercise aids in calorie burning, promotes the development of lean muscle mass, and boosts metabolism, thereby contributing to weight loss or weight maintenance.

4. Insulin Sensitivity and Diabetes Management: Physical activity enhances insulin sensitivity, which is particularly beneficial for individuals with diabetes or those at risk of developing type 2 diabetes. When combined with the DASH diet, exercise helps regulate blood sugar levels, improves glycemic control, and lowers the likelihood of diabetes-related complications.

5. Mental and Emotional Well-being: Participating in physical activity triggers the release of endorphins, which promote feelings of happiness and well-being. Regular exercise has been associated with reduced stress levels, improved mood, enhanced cognitive function, and overall mental well-being. The integration of physical activity into the DASH lifestyle can have a positive impact on both physical and mental health.

6. Bone Health: Weight-bearing exercises like walking, jogging, dancing, or weightlifting contribute to improved bone density and strength. Incorporating physical activity into the DASH lifestyle helps maintain healthy bones & decreases the risk of osteoporosis.

7. Energy Balance: Regular exercise supports a healthy energy balance by burning calories and promoting a well-functioning metabolism. When combined with the nutrient-rich DASH diet, physical activity encourages a balanced approach to energy intake and expenditure.

8. Long-term Health Maintenance: Physical activity is an indispensable component of a healthy lifestyle. By incorporating regular exercise into the DASH lifestyle, individuals can foster long-term health maintenance and decrease the risks of chronic diseases such as heart disease, obesity, type 2 diabetes, & certain types of cancer.

Transitioning into Recipes

Transitioning into the DASH diet recipes can be a gradual process that allows you to adapt to the new eating pattern. Below are some steps to help you transition smoothly:

1. Familiarize Yourself with DASH Guidelines: Prior to diving into specific recipes, familiarize yourself with the DASH diet guidelines. Understand the recommended food groups, portion sizes, and nutrient goals. This will give you the information you need to make smart food choices.

2. Start with Small Changes: Start by making small changes to the way you eat now. Gradually increase your intake of fruits, vegetables, whole grains, and lean proteins while reducing high-sodium and processed foods. For example, incorporate a side salad or vegetable dish with your

meals, choose whole grain bread instead of white bread, or swap out a high-sodium snack for a piece of fruit.

3. Explore DASH-Friendly Recipes: Look for DASH diet recipes that appeal to you. There are numerous online resources, cookbooks, and websites dedicated to DASH-friendly meals. Start incorporating these recipes into your weekly meal plan gradually.

4. Meal Planning and Preparation: Plan your meals in advance to ensure you have DASH-compliant options readily available. Experiment with recipes that feature a variety of fruits, vegetables, whole grains, and lean proteins. Prepare larger batches of meals and store leftovers for convenience during busy days.

5. Increase Fruit and Vegetable Intake: Focus on increasing your daily intake of fruits and vegetables. Aim for a variety of colors & types to ensure a wide range of nutrients. Incorporate them into meals, snacks, smoothies, and salads. Gradually increase the number of servings over time.

6. Opt for Whole Grains: Try whole grains instead of processed carbs. Instead of their refined versions, choose whole wheat bread, brown rice, whole grain pasta, and oats. Experiment with different grains like quinoa, bulgur, and barley to diversify your meals.

7. Diminish Sodium Intake: Gradually diminish your sodium intake by cutting back on processed & packaged foods, which are typically high in sodium. Cook meals from scratch utilizing fresh components and herbs and spices to include flavor as an alternative of relying on salt.

8. Seek Inspiration and Support: Join online communities, forums, or social media groups dedicated to the DASH diet. Engage with others who are following or have transitioned into the DASH lifestyle. Share experiences, ask questions, and seek recipe ideas. Drawing inspiration and support from others can make the transition easier.

9. Monitor Your Progress: Keep track of your dietary changes and monitor how your body responds to the DASH diet. Pay attention to any improvements in blood pressure, energy levels, weight, or overall well-being. This can serve as motivation and reinforcement for sticking to the DASH lifestyle.

Remember, transitioning to any new eating pattern takes time and patience. It's essential to listen to your body, adapt recipes to suit your taste preferences, and consult with healthcare professionals or registered dietitians for personalized guidance and support throughout the process.

CHAPTER 1
BREAKFAST

1. Whole Grain Breakfast Burrito	17
2. Yogurt and Berry Smoothie	17
3. Overnight Chia Pudding	17
4. Sweet Potato Hash with Eggs	18
5. Green Smoothie Bowl	18
6. Banana Pancakes	18
7. Cottage Cheese and Fruit Bowl	19
8. Chia Seed Pudding with Berries	19
9. Quinoa Breakfast Bowl	19
10. Avocado and Egg Toast	20
11. Spinach and Feta Omelette	20
12. Smoked Salmon Breakfast Toast	20
13. Spinach and Feta Breakfast Wrap	21
14. Smashed Avocado Toast	21
15. Berry Chia Pudding	21

1. Whole Grain Breakfast Burrito

Preparation time: ten mins

Cooking time: ten mins

Servings: 2

Ingredients:

- 2 whole grain tortillas
- 4 big eggs
- quarter teacup severed mixed vegetables (e.g., bell peppers, onions, spinach)
- quarter teacup shredded low-fat cheese
- Salt and pepper as required
- Optional toppings: salsa, avocado, Greek yogurt

Directions:

1. Inside your container, beat the eggs with salt and pepper.
2. Inside a non-stick griddle, sauté the mixed vegetables till soft.
3. Pour the beaten eggs into the griddle then scramble till cooked through.
4. Warm the tortillas in another griddle or microwave.
5. On each tortilla, put some scrambled eggs.
6. Spray with shredded cheese and include optional toppings.
7. Roll up the tortillas to form burritos.
8. Serve warm.

Per serving: Calories: 300 kcal; Fat: 14g; Carbs: 24g; Protein: 20g; Sodium: 440mg; Potassium: 250mg; Phosphorus: 220mg; Calcium: 200mg; Magnesium: 40mg

2. Yogurt and Berry Smoothie

Preparation time: five mins

Cooking time: zero mins

Servings: one

Ingredients:

- half teacup plain low-fat yogurt
- half teacup unsweetened almond milk
- half teacup mixed berries (e.g., strawberries, blueberries)
- half ripe banana
- one tbsp honey or maple syrup
- half teacup ice cubes

Directions:

1. Inside a mixer, blend the entire components.
2. Blend till level and creamy.
3. Pour into a glass and serve chilled.

Per serving: Calories: 180 kcal; Fat: 3g; Carbs: 34g; Protein: 8g; Sodium: 110mg; Potassium: 380mg; Phosphorus: 200mg; Calcium: 250mg; Magnesium: 30mg

3. Overnight Chia Pudding

Preparation time: five mins

Cooking time: zero mins

Servings: two

Ingredients:

- one teacup unsweetened almond milk
- quarter teacup chia seeds
- one tbsp honey or maple syrup
- half tsp vanilla extract
- Toppings: sliced fresh fruit, nuts, seeds

Directions:

1. Inside your container, whisk simultaneously almond milk, chia seeds, honey or maple syrup, and vanilla extract.
2. Allow the solution sit for five mins, whisking occasionally to prevent clumping.
3. Place a lid on the container and place it into the fridge for around four hrs or overnight till it becomes thicker.
4. Prior to serving, give the chia pudding a good stir.
5. Divide the pudding into two servings and top with sliced fresh fruit, nuts, and seeds.
6. Enjoy chilled.

Per serving: Calories: 180 kcal; Fat: 9g; Carbs: 16g; Protein: 6g; Sodium: 70mg; Potassium: 200mg; Phosphorus: 180mg; Calcium: 250mg; Magnesium: 80mg

4. Sweet Potato Hash with Eggs

Preparation time: ten mins

Cooking time: twenty mins

Servings: two

Ingredients:

- one big sweet potato, skinned and cubed
- one small onion, cubed
- one red bell pepper, cubed
- two pieces garlic, crushed
- two tbsps olive oil
- half tsp paprika
- Salt and pepper as required
- 4 big eggs

Directions:

1. Warm the olive oil in a griddle across moderate flame.
2. Include the sweet potato, onion, bell pepper, and garlic.
3. Season with paprika, salt, and pepper.
4. Sauté for ten-fifteen mins till the sweet potato is soft and mildly browned.
5. Make four wells in the hash then crack an egg into every well.
6. Cover the griddle then cook for 5-7 mins 'til the eggs are cooked to your liking.
7. Serve warm.

Per serving: Calories: 350 kcal; Fat: 18g; Carbs: 34g; Protein: 15g; Sodium: 180mg; Potassium: 850mg; Phosphorus: 270mg; Calcium: 70mg; Magnesium: 60mg

5. Green Smoothie Bowl

Preparation time: five mins

Cooking time: zero mins

Servings: one

Ingredients:

- one frozen banana
- one teacup baby spinach or kale
- half teacup unsweetened almond milk
- quarter teacup plain low-fat yogurt
- one tbsp almond butter or peanut butter
- Toppings: sliced fresh fruit, granola, chia seeds

Directions:

1. Inside a mixer, blend the frozen banana, baby spinach or kale, almond milk, yogurt, and almond butter.
2. Blend till level and creamy.
3. Pour into a container then top with sliced fresh fruit, granola, and chia seeds.
4. Serve chilled.

Per serving: Calories: 300 kcal; Fat: 12g; Carbs: 42g; Protein: 10g; Sodium: 230mg; Potassium: 860mg; Phosphorus: 300mg; Calcium: 300mg; Magnesium: 130mg

6. Banana Pancakes

Preparation time: ten mins

Cooking time: ten mins

Servings: two

Ingredients:

- one teacup flour
- one ripe banana, pounded
- one egg
- one teacup low-fat milk
- one tbsp honey
- one tsp baking powder
- half tsp cinnamon
- Cooking spray

Directions:

1. Inside your container, mix simultaneously the flour, baking powder, and cinnamon.
2. In separate container, mix the mashed banana, egg, milk, and honey utilizing a whisk.
3. Blend the wet and dry components simultaneously, blending till they are just combined.
4. Warm up a non-stick griddle or griddle on moderate flame and apply a coat of cooking spray.
5. Use quarter teacup of the batter per pancake then pour it onto the griddle.
6. Continue cooking for two to three mins on both ends till they turn golden brown.

7. Replicate with the remaining batter.

8. Serve warm with your choice of toppings (e.g., fresh fruit, yogurt).

Per serving: Calories: 280 kcal; Fat: 3g; Carbs: 57g; Protein: 11g; Sodium: 180mg; Potassium: 470mg; Phosphorus: 280mg; Calcium: 220mg; Magnesium: 50mg

7. Cottage Cheese and Fruit Bowl

Preparation time: five mins

Cooking time: zero mins

Servings: one

Ingredients:

- half teacup low-fat cottage cheese
- half teacup mixed fresh fruit (e.g., pineapple, kiwi, grapes)
- one tbsp severed nuts (e.g., walnuts, almonds)
- one tbsp honey

Directions:

1. Inside your container, spoon the cottage cheese.

2. Top with mixed fresh fruit and severed nuts.

3. Spray with honey.

4. Serve chilled.

Per serving: Calories: 200 kcal; Fat: 6gm; Carbs: 20g; Protein: 16gm; Sodium: 360mg; Potassium: 270mg; Phosphorus: 210mg; Calcium: 150mg; Magnesium: 30mg

8. Chia Seed Pudding with Berries

Preparation time: five mins

Cooking time: zero mins

Servings: two

Ingredients:

- one teacup unsweetened almond milk
- quarter teacup chia seeds
- one tbsp honey or maple syrup
- half tsp vanilla extract
- half teacup fresh berries (e.g., strawberries, raspberries)
- two tbsps sliced almonds

Directions:

1. Inside your container, whisk simultaneously almond milk, chia seeds, honey or maple syrup, and vanilla extract.

2. Allow the solution sit for 5 mins, whisking occasionally to prevent clumping.

3. Cover the container then put in the fridge for around four hrs or overnight till densed.

4. Prior to serving, give the chia pudding a good stir.

5. Divide the pudding into two servings and top with fresh berries and sliced almonds.

6. Enjoy chilled.

Per serving: Calories: 200 kcal; Fat: 12g; Carbs: 19g; Protein: 6g; Sodium: 70mg; Potassium: 190mg; Phosphorus: 160mg; Calcium: 200mg; Magnesium: 70mg

9. Quinoa Breakfast Bowl

Preparation time: five mins

Cooking time: fifteen mins

Servings: two

Ingredients:

- one teacup cooked quinoa
- half teacup low-fat milk
- quarter teacup unsweetened Greek yogurt
- one tbsp honey
- quarter teacup fresh berries (e.g., raspberries, blackberries)
- one tbsp severed nuts (e.g., pistachios, almonds)
- half tsp vanilla extract

Directions:

1. In a small saucepot, temp. the cooked quinoa with the milk and vanilla extract across moderate flame till warmed through.

2. Divide the quinoa solution into two containers.

3. Top each container with Greek yogurt, fresh berries, severed nuts, and spray with honey.

4. Serve warm.

Per serving: Calories: 250 kcal; Fat: 6gm; Carbs: 42g; Protein: 10gm; Sodium: 70mg; Potassium: 300mg; Phosphorus: 150mg; Calcium: 200mg; Magnesium: 70mg

10. Avocado and Egg Toast

Preparation time: five mins

Cooking time: five mins

Servings: one

Ingredients:

- one slice whole grain bread, toasted
- half ripe avocado, mashed
- one big egg, fried or poached
- Salt and pepper as required
- Optional toppings: cherry tomatoes, sprouts, red pepper flakes

Directions:

1. Take the toasted bread and apply the mashed avocado uniformly.

2. Top with a fried or poached egg.

3. Season with salt and pepper.

4. Include optional toppings if anticipated.

5. Serve warm.

Per serving: Calories: 300 kcal; Fat: 15g; Carbs: 27g; Protein: 15g; Sodium: 240mg; Potassium: 560mg; Phosphorus: 170mg; Calcium: 60mg; Magnesium: 40mg

11. Spinach and Feta Omelette

Preparation time: ten mins

Cooking time: five mins

Servings: one

Ingredients:

- two big eggs
- half teacup fresh spinach, severed
- two tbsps crumbled feta cheese
- Salt and pepper as required

Directions:

1. Inside your container, beat the eggs with salt and pepper.

2. Warm a griddle that is non-stick on moderate flame and apply a thin layer of cooking spray to it.

3. Include the severed spinach and sauté for one to two mins till wilted.

4. Pour the beaten eggs over the spinach and let cook for two to three mins.

5. Spray the feta cheese on top and fold the omelette in half.

6. Continue cooking for one to two mins till the cheese has completely dissolved.

7. Serve warm.

Per serving: Calories: 250 kcal; Fat: 18g; Carbs: 3g; Protein: 19g; Sodium: 420mg; Potassium: 400mg; Phosphorus: 300mg; Calcium: 200mg; Magnesium: 50mg

12. Smoked Salmon Breakfast Toast

Preparation time: five mins

Cooking time: zero mins

Servings: one

Ingredients:

- one slice whole grain bread, toasted
- two tbsps low-fat cream cheese
- two oz. smoked salmon
- one tbsp capers
- one tbsp severed fresh dill
- Lemon wedges for serving

Directions:

1. Disperse the cream cheese uniformly on the toasted bread.

2. Top with smoked salmon.

3. Spray with capers and severed fresh dill.

4. Lemon pieces should be on the side.

Per serving: Calories: 250 kcal; Fat: 10g; Carbs: 20g; Protein: 20g; Sodium: 550mg; Potassium: 180mg; Phosphorus: 190mg; Calcium: 80mg; Magnesium: 25mg

13. Spinach and Feta Breakfast Wrap

Preparation time: five mins

Cooking time: five mins

Servings: one

Ingredients:

- one tortilla
- half teacup fresh spinach leaves
- two big eggs, scrambled
- two tbsps crumbled feta cheese
- Salt and pepper as required
- Cooking spray

Directions:

1. First, warm a griddle that is non-stick on moderate flame, and then apply a thin layer of cooking spray.
2. Place the tortilla in the griddle and warm for a couple of secs on every end.
3. In the same griddle, cook the scrambled eggs till they are set.
4. Add salt and pepper to the eggs.
5. Lay the tortilla onto a plate and arrange the fresh spinach leaves on top.
6. Spoon the scrambled eggs onto the spinach.
7. Spray with crumbled feta cheese.
8. Roll up the tortilla to form a wrap.
9. Serve warm.

Per serving: Calories: 300 kcal; Fat: 15g; Carbs: 22g; Protein: 20g; Sodium: 450mg; Potassium: 300mg; Phosphorus: 260mg; Calcium: 200mg; Magnesium: 60mg

14. Smashed Avocado Toast

Preparation time: five mins

Cooking time: zero mins

Servings: one

Ingredients:

- one slice whole grain bread, toasted
- half ripe avocado, smashed
- one tsp lemon juice
- Salt and pepper as required
- Optional toppings: sliced tomatoes, sprouts, feta cheese

Directions:

1. Apply the crushed avocado onto the bread that has been toasted.
2. Spray with lemon juice then spray with salt and pepper.
3. Include your anticipated toppings.
4. Serve instantly.

Per serving: Calories: 200 kcal; Fat: 14g; Carbs: 18g; Protein: 4g; Sodium: 120mg; Potassium: 500mg; Phosphorus: 100mg; Calcium: 20mg; Magnesium: 20mg

15. Berry Chia Pudding

Preparation time: five mins

Cooking time: zero mins

Servings: two

Ingredients:

- one teacup unsweetened almond milk
- quarter teacup chia seeds
- one tbsp honey or maple syrup
- half tsp vanilla extract
- half teacup mixed berries (e.g., strawberries, blueberries)

Directions:

1. Inside your container, whisk simultaneously almond milk, chia seeds, honey or maple syrup, and vanilla extract.
2. Allow the solution sit for five mins, whisking occasionally to prevent clumping.
3. Cover the container then put in the fridge for around 4 hrs or overnight till densed.
4. Prior to serving, give the chia pudding a good stir.
5. Divide the pudding into two servings and top with mixed berries.
6. Enjoy chilled.

Per serving: Calories: 170 kcal; Fat: 9g; Carbs: 16g; Protein: 5g; Sodium: 90mg; Potassium: 200mg; Phosphorus: 150mg; Calcium: 250mg; Magnesium: 90mg

CHAPTER 2
LUNCH

16. Chicken Chop Suey 23

17. Caprese Salad 23

18. Pork and Pumpkin Chili 23

19. Caprese Pasta Salad 24

20. Lentil and Vegetable Soup 24

21. Turkey and Avocado Wrap 25

22. Ground Beef and Bell Peppers 25

23. Pork Chops and Apples 25

24. Greek Quinoa Salad 26

25. Mediterranean Tuna Salad 26

26. Tuna Salad Lettuce Wraps 26

27. Oven Fried Chicken 27

28. Greek Chickpea Salad 27

29. Greek Turkey Burgers 27

30. Cajun Pork Chops 28

16. Chicken Chop Suey

Preparation time: ten mins

Cooking time: twenty mins

Servings: 3

Ingredients:

- two tsps olive oil
- quarter tsp dried tarragon
- quarter tsp dried marjoram
- quarter tsp dried basil
- quarter tsp grated lemon zest
- one and half tbsps low-sodium teriyaki sauce
- ¼ cup pineapple tidbits
- one and half tbsps unsweetened pineapple juice
- one tbsp cornstarch
- half lb. boneless skinless chicken breasts, cut into one-inch pieces (two and half cm)
- ¾ cup severed carrots
- ½ can (from 8oz) sliced water chestnuts, drained
- ¼ cup severed onion
- ½ medium tart apple, cored, severed
- ½ cup cold water, divided
- 1 ½ cups hot cooked brown rice

Directions:

1. Put a pot on flame, include oil to it and let it temp.. Pour oil into it then let it temp.. Once the oil is heated, place the chicken in your griddle.

1. Spray lemon zest and the dry herbs and cook till the chicken is light brown. Include carrots, apple, water chestnut, onion, and pineapple and stir.

2. Include teriyaki sauce, pineapple juice, and half the water and stir. Lower the flame and cook till the chicken gets mushy or when it begins to boil. Whisk simultaneously the remaining water and cornstarch in a container and pour into the griddle. Stir constantly till thick. Let it come back to a boil.

3. To serve: Place ½ cup of rice on each plate. Spoon chicken chop Suey across the rice and serve.

Per serving: Calories: 221kcal; Carbs: 0.9g; Protein: 11gm; Fat: 17g; Sodium: 180mg; Potassium: 320mg; Phosphorus: 280mg; Calcium: 15mg; Magnesium: 35mg

17. Caprese Salad

Preparation time: fifteen mins

Cooking time: zero mins

Servings: four

Ingredients:

- two big tomatoes, sliced
- 8 oz fresh mozzarella cheese, sliced
- one teacup fresh basil leaves
- two tbsps balsamic glaze
- two tbsps extra virgin olive oil
- Salt and pepper as required

Directions:

1. Place the tomato slices neatly onto a serving platter.

2. On top of each slice of tomato, put a piece of fresh mozzarella.

3. Top each mozzarella slice with a fresh basil leaf.

4. Spray the balsamic glaze and extra virgin olive oil across the tomato, mozzarella, and basil.

5. Season with salt and pepper as required.

6. Serve instantly and relish!

Per serving: Calories: 220 kcal; Fat: 17g; Carbs: 6g; Protein: 10g; Sodium: 300mg; Potassium: 380mg; Phosphorus: 190mg; Calcium: 250mg; Magnesium: 30mg

18. Pork and Pumpkin Chili

Preparation time: ten mins

Cooking time: one hr and thirty mins

Servings: 6

Ingredients:

- one green bell pepper, severed
- two teacups yellow onion, severed
- one tbsp olive oil
- 6 garlic pieces, crushed
- 2eight oz. canned tomatoes, no-salt-included and severed
- half-pounds pork, ground

- 6 ounces low-sodium tomato paste
- 14 ounces pumpkin puree
- one teacup low-sodium chicken stock
- 2 and half tsps oregano, dried
- 1 and half tsp cinnamon, ground
- 1 and half tablespoon chili powder
- Black pepper as required

Directions:

1. Warm a pot with the oil on a moderate-high flame, include bell peppers and onion, stir and cook for 7 mins. Include garlic and the pork, toss and cook for ten mins.

2. Include tomatoes, tomato paste, pumpkin puree, stock, oregano, cinnamon, chili powder and pepper, stir, cover, cook across moderate flame for one hr and ten mins, split into containers and serve.

Per serving: Calories: 276kcal; Carbs: 36g; Protein: 11.5g; Fat: 10g; Sodium: 339mg; Potassium: 685mg; Phosphorus: 419mg; Calcium: 25mg; Magnesium: 30mg

19. Caprese Pasta Salad

Preparation time: fifteen mins

Cooking time: ten mins

Servings: four

Ingredients:

- eight oz. penne pasta
- one teacup cherry tomatoes, shared
- one teacup fresh mozzarella balls, shared
- quarter teacup severed fresh basil
- two tbsps extra virgin olive oil
- two tbsps balsamic vinegar
- one clove garlic, crushed
- Salt and pepper as required

Directions:

1. Prepare the penne pasta by following the instructions on the package till it reaches the anticipated firmness. Once the pasta is done, drain it and put it away.

2. Inside a huge container, blend the cooked penne pasta, cherry tomatoes,

fresh mozzarella balls, severed fresh basil, extra virgin olive oil, balsamic vinegar, crushed garlic, salt, and pepper. Toss everything simultaneously till well combined and uniformly coated.

3. Put in the fridge for around one hr prior to serving to let the flavors to meld.

4. Serve the caprese pasta salad chilled as a delicious and satisfying lunch option.

5. Enjoy!

Per serving: Calories: 310 kcal; Fat: 14g; Carbs: 32g; Protein: 15g; Sodium: 200mg; Potassium: 270mg; Phosphorus: 190mg; Calcium: 200mg; Magnesium: 30mg

20. Lentil and Vegetable Soup

Preparation time: fifteen mins

Cooking time: thirty mins

Servings: four

Ingredients:

- one teacup dried lentils, washed
- one carrot, cubed
- one celery stalk, cubed
- half onion, cubed
- two pieces garlic, crushed
- four teacups low-sodium vegetable broth
- one teacup cubed tomatoes (canned or fresh)
- one tsp dried thyme
- half tsp dried oregano
- Salt and pepper as required
- Fresh parsley for garnish

Directions:

1. Inside a big pot, blend the dried lentils, cubed carrot, cubed celery, cubed onion, crushed garlic, vegetable broth, cubed tomatoes, dried thyme, dried oregano, salt, and pepper.

2. Boil across moderate-high flame.

3. Lower the temp., cover the pot, afterwards simmer for about 25-thirty mins or 'til the lentils and vegetables are soft.

4. Season with extra salt & pepper if required.
5. Ladle the lentil and vegetable soup into containers.
6. Garnish with fresh parsley.
7. Serve the soup hot and relish!

Per serving: Calories: 200 kcal; Fat: 1g; Carbs: 37g; Protein: 14g; Sodium: 480mg; Potassium: 680mg; Phosphorus: 270mg; Calcium: 60mg; Magnesium: 50mg

21. Turkey and Avocado Wrap

Preparation time: fifteen mins

Cooking time: zero mins

Servings: four

Ingredients:

- 4 tortillas or wraps
- 8 slices turkey breast
- 1 avocado, sliced
- half teacup baby spinach leaves
- quarter teacup sliced red onion
- two tbsps Greek yogurt
- one tbsp Dijon mustard
- Salt and pepper as required

Directions:

1. Lay out the tortillas or wraps on a clean surface.
2. Disperse half tablespoon of Greek yogurt and 1/4 tablespoon of Dijon mustard on each tortilla or wrap.
3. Place 2 slices of turkey breast on each tortilla or wrap.
4. Top with avocado slices, baby spinach leaves, and sliced red onion.
5. Season with salt and pepper as required.
6. Roll up the tortillas or wraps tightly, enclosing the fillings.
7. Slice the wraps in half, if anticipated, and serve.
8. Enjoy!

Per serving: Calories: 250 kcal; Fat: 10g; Carbs: 24g; Protein: 15g; Sodium: 480mg; Potassium: 380mg; Phosphorus: 230mg; Calcium: 50mg; Magnesium: 30mg

22. Ground Beef and Bell Peppers

Preparation time: ten mins

Cooking time: ten mins

Servings: two

Ingredients:

- one teacup spinach (severed)
- one onion (severed)
- one tbsp coconut oil
- 0.5-lb. ground beef
- one red bell pepper (cubed)
- quarter tsp salt
- quarter tsp black pepper

Directions:

1. Inside a pot, blend the onion and coconut oil, and sauté across moderate-high flame till the onion is gently browned.
2. Include the spinach, salt, and ground meat after that.
3. Stir fry till everything is done. Meanwhile, remove all of the seeds from the interior of the red bell pepper.
4. After that, remove the solution from the pot and spoon it into the bell pepper. Serve.

Per serving: Calories: 357kcal; Carbs: 7.89g; Protein: 31.68g; Fat: 19.61g; Sodium: 136mg; Potassium: 668mg; Phosphorus: 215mg; Calcium: 52mg; Magnesium: 54mg

23. Pork Chops and Apples

Preparation time: ten mins

Cooking time: one hr

Servings: four

Ingredients:

- one and half teacups chicken stock
- Black pepper as required
- 4 pork chops
- one yellow onion, severed
- one tbsp olive oil
- two garlic pieces, crushed
- 3 apples, cored and sliced
- one tbsp thyme, severed

Directions:

1. Warm a pot with the oil across moderate-high flame, include pork chops, season with black pepper and cook for five mins.

2. Include onion, garlic, apples, thyme and stock, toss, include in the oven then bake at 350 deg. F for fifty mins. Divide everything among plates and serve.

Per serving: Calories: 332kcal; Carbs: 50g; Protein: 7.4g; Fat: 13.7g; Sodium: 226mg; Potassium: 675mg; Phosphorus: 440mg; Calcium: 35mg; Magnesium: 35mg

24. Greek Quinoa Salad

Preparation time: fifteen mins

Cooking time: fifteen mins

Servings: four

Ingredients:

- one teacup cooked quinoa
- one teacup cherry tomatoes, shared
- one cucumber, cubed
- half teacup cubed red onion
- quarter teacup sliced Kalamata olives
- quarter teacup crumbled feta cheese
- two tbsps extra virgin olive oil
- two tbsps lemon juice
- one tbsp severed fresh parsley
- Salt and pepper as required

Directions:

1. Inside a huge container, blend the cooked quinoa, cherry tomatoes, cubed cucumber, cubed red onion, sliced Kalamata olives, crumbled feta cheese, olive oil, lemon juice, severed parsley, salt, and pepper.

2. Toss everything simultaneously till well combined and uniformly coated.

3. Allow the flavors to blend by refrigerating for one hour prior to serving.

4. Serve the Greek quinoa salad chilled as a refreshing and nutritious lunch option.

5. Enjoy!

Per serving: Calories: 250 kcal; Fat: 14g; Carbs: 25g; Protein: 7g; Sodium: 420mg; Potassium: 400mg; Phosphorus: 190mg; Calcium: 80mg; Magnesium: 60mg

25. Mediterranean Tuna Salad

Preparation time: fifteen mins

Cooking time: zero mins

Servings: four

Ingredients:

- 2 cans tuna in water, drained
- one teacup cubed cucumber
- half teacup cubed tomatoes
- quarter teacup sliced Kalamata olives
- quarter teacup cubed red onion
- two tbsps severed fresh parsley
- two tbsps lemon juice
- two tbsps extra virgin olive oil
- Salt and pepper as required

Directions:

1. Inside a huge container, blend the drained tuna, cubed cucumber, cubed tomatoes, sliced Kalamata olives, cubed red onion, severed fresh parsley, lemon juice, extra virgin olive oil, salt, and pepper. Mix thoroughly to blend the entire components.

2. Put in the fridge for around one hr prior to serving to allow the flavors to meld.

3. Serve the Mediterranean tuna salad chilled as a light and satisfying lunch option.

4. Enjoy!

Per serving: Calories: 180 kcal; Fat: 10g; Carbs: 7g; Protein: 16g; Sodium: 480mg; Potassium: 370mg; Phosphorus: 180mg; Calcium: 50mg; Magnesium: 40mg

26. Tuna Salad Lettuce Wraps

Preparation time: fifteen mins

Cooking time: zero mins

Servings: four

Ingredients:

- quarter teacup cubed red onion
- quarter teacup cubed celery
- quarter teacup cubed cucumber
- two tbsps mayonnaise

- one tbsp lemon juice
- Salt and pepper as required
- two cans (5 oz each) tuna in water, drained
- 8 big lettuce leaves (such as romaine or butter lettuce)

Directions:

1. Inside your container, blend the drained tuna, cubed red onion, cubed celery, cubed cucumber, mayonnaise, lemon juice, salt, and pepper. Mix thoroughly to blend the entire components.

2. Spoon the tuna salad solution onto the center of each lettuce leaf.

3. Roll up the lettuce leaves, enclosing the tuna salad.

4. Serve the tuna salad lettuce wraps as a refreshing and light lunch option.

5. Enjoy!

Per serving: Calories: 150 kcal; Fat: 6g; Carbs: 3g; Protein: 20g; Sodium: 280mg; Potassium: 190mg; Phosphorus: 140mg; Calcium: 30mg; Magnesium: 20mg

27. Oven Fried Chicken

Preparation time: ten mins

Cooking time: sixty mins

Servings: 14

Ingredients:

- one 3-lbs. broiled-fryer chicken (cut up)
- half teacup flour
- quarter teacup shortening
- quarter teacup margarine
- one tsp paprika
- half tsp pepper
- half tsp onion powder

Directions:

3. Warm up the oven to 425 deg. F. Wash the chicken and pat it dry. Melt shortening and margarine in a thirteen by nine by two inch baking pot in the oven.

4. Combine flour, paprika, pepper, and onion powder in a medium mixing basin. Coat the chicken pieces in the flour solution completely. Put the skin side of the chicken in the dissolved shortening.

5. Cook for thirty mins, uncovered. Cook for another thirty mins or 'til the thickest parts are fork-soft.

Per serving: Calories: 184kcal; Carbs: 2g; Protein: 21g; Fat: 10g; Sodium: 136mg; Potassium: 101mg; Phosphorus: 100mg; Calcium: 0mg; Magnesium: 0mg

28. Greek Chickpea Salad

Preparation time: fifteen mins

Cooking time: zero mins

Servings: four

Ingredients:

- two tins chickpeas, washed and drained
- one cucumber, cubed
- half red onion, finely sliced
- one teacup cherry tomatoes, shared
- quarter teacup sliced Kalamata olives
- quarter teacup crumbled feta cheese
- two tbsps severed fresh parsley
- two tbsps lemon juice
- two tbsps extra virgin olive oil
- Salt and pepper as required

Directions:

1. Inside a huge container, blend the chickpeas, cubed cucumber, finely cutred onion, cherry tomatoes, sliced Kalamata olives, crumbled feta cheese, severed fresh lemon juice, parsley, extra virgin olive oil, salt, & pepper. Mix thoroughly to blend the entire components.

2. Put in the fridge for around one hr prior to serving to allow the flavors to meld.

3. Serve the Greek chickpea salad chilled as a healthy and flavorful lunch option.

4. Enjoy!

Per serving: Calories: 290 kcal; Fat: 13g; Carbs: 34g; Protein: 12g; Sodium: 540mg; Potassium: 500mg; Phosphorus: 190mg; Calcium: 130mg; Magnesium: 60mg

29. Greek Turkey Burgers

Preparation time: fifteen mins

Cooking time: fifteen mins

Servings: four

Ingredients:

- one lb. ground turkey
- quarter teacup crumbled feta cheese
- quarter teacup severed fresh spinach
- two tbsps severed fresh parsley
- two tbsps severed red onion
- one clove garlic, crushed
- one tsp dried oregano
- Salt and pepper as required
- 4 burger buns
- Toppings of choice (e.g., lettuce, tomato, red onion)

Directions:

1. Inside your container, blend the ground turkey, feta cheese, spinach, parsley, red onion, crushed garlic, dried oregano, salt, and pepper. Mix thoroughly to incorporate all the components.
2. After dividing the solution into 4 similar parts, proceed to shape each portion into burger patties.
3. Warm up a grill or griddle across moderate flame.
4. Cook the turkey burgers for around six to seven mins per side or 'til they reach an internal temp. of 165 deg. F.
5. Toast the whole temp. Once the pasta is done, drain it and put it away.
6. Place the cooked turkey burgers on the toasted buns and include your anticipated toppings.
7. Serve and relish!

Per serving: Calories: 300 kcal; Fat: 10g; Carbs: 26g; Protein: 25g; Sodium: 400mg; Potassium: 350mg; Phosphorus: 220mg; Calcium: 100mg; Magnesium: 40mg

30. Cajun Pork Chops

Preparation time: ten mins

Cooking time: thirty-six mins

Servings: four

Ingredients:

- quarter tsp paprika
- quarter tsp thyme
- quarter tsp dry mustard
- quarter tsp ground sage
- quarter tsp ground cumin
- quarter tsp garlic powder
- four pork chops cut half-inch thick (four oz each)
- one small onion (sliced)
- one-eighth tsp pepper
- one tbsp margarine
- one tsp parsley flakes
- one-eighth tsp garlic powder
- two to three drops of hot pepper sauce

Directions:

1. On a piece of waxed paper, mix together a quarter teaspoon of garlic powder, paprika, thyme, mustard, sage, cumin, and pepper. Coat both sides of the pork chops with the sauce.
2. Place chops in a single layer on an 8-inch square dish that can go in the microwave.
3. Put the onion slices place on top of each chop. Use the waxed paper to cover the dish. Microwave for five mins on high.
4. Microwave on low (30%) for 25 to thirty mins or till vegetables are soft, turning once throughout this time. Allow resting while you prepare the sauce.
5. Combine margarine, parsley, one-eighth tsp garlic powder, and pepper sauce in a small glass container. Microwave for thirty to forty secs on high, or till dissolved.
6. Prior to serving, spray the sauce across the chops.

Per serving: Calories: 243kcal; Carbs: 3g; Protein: 22g; Fat: 16g; Sodium: 116mg; Potassium: 432mg; Phosphorus: 367mg; Calcium: 24mg; Magnesium: 32mg

CHAPTER 3
DINNER

31. TURKEY MEATBALLS WITH PASTA   30

32. GRILLED VEGGIE AND HALLOUMI SKEWERS   30

33. BAKED COD WITH LEMON-HERB QUINOA   31

34. VEGETABLE LENTIL SOUP   31

35. SPICED UP PORK CHOPS   31

36. BAKED SALMON WITH QUINOA AND ROASTED VEGETABLES   32

37. SALMON WITH QUINOA AND STEAMED BROCCOLI   32

38. PORK AND SWEET POTATOES   33

39. TURKEY AND VEGETABLE STIR-FRY   33

40. PORK WITH DATES SAUCE   33

41. GRILLED CHICKEN WITH ROASTED SWEET POTATOES AND GREEN BEANS   34

42. BAKED COD WITH QUINOA AND STEAMED ASPARAGUS   34

43. LENTIL AND VEGETABLE CURRY   34

44. CHICKEN STIR-FRY WITH BROWN RICE   35

45. HERBED BUTTER PORK CHOPS   35

31. Turkey Meatballs with Pasta

Preparation time: fifteen mins

Cooking time: twenty-five mins

Servings: four

Ingredients:

- 1 lb. ground turkey
- half teacup breadcrumbs
- quarter teacup grated Parmesan cheese
- quarter teacup severed fresh parsley
- 1 egg, beaten
- two pieces garlic, crushed
- half tsp dried oregano
- half tsp dried basil
- Salt and pepper as required
- 8 oz pasta
- two teacups marinara sauce
- Chopped fresh basil for garnish

Directions:

1. Inside a huge container, blend the ground turkey, breadcrumbs, grated Parmesan cheese, severed fresh parsley, beaten egg, crushed garlic, dried oregano, dried basil, salt, and pepper. Mix thoroughly.
2. Form the solution into meatballs.
3. Inside a huge griddle, temp. olive oil across moderate flame. Include the meatballs then cook for 8-ten mins 'til browned on all sides and cooked through.
4. Prepare the pasta by following the instructions provided on the packaging. Drain and put away.
5. In a distinct saucepot, warm the marinara sauce over low temp.
6. Serve the turkey meatballs over cooked pasta, topped with marinara sauce. Garnish with severed fresh basil prior to serving.

Per serving: Calories: 380 kcal; Fat: 10g; Carbs: 45g; Protein: 30g; Sodium: 500mg; Potassium: 400mg; Phosphorus: 250mg; Calcium: 100mg; Magnesium: 50mg

32. Grilled Veggie and Halloumi Skewers

Preparation time: fifteen mins

Cooking time: ten mins

Servings: four

Ingredients:

- one zucchini, cut into thick slices
- one yellow squash, cut into thick slices
- one red onion, cut into wedges
- one red bell pepper, cut into chunks
- one yellow bell pepper, cut into chunks
- 8 oz halloumi cheese, cut into cubes
- two tbsps olive oil
- one tbsp balsamic vinegar
- one tsp dried oregano
- Wooden skewers, soaked in water for thirty mins
- Salt and pepper as required

Directions:

1. Warm up the grill to moderate-high flame.
2. Inside a huge container, blend the zucchini, yellow squash, red onion, red bell pepper, yellow bell pepper, halloumi cheese, olive oil, balsamic vinegar, dried oregano, salt, and pepper. Toss well to coat.
3. Thread the vegetables and halloumi cheese onto the wooden skewers, alternating among the various components.
4. Grill the skewers for 8 to 10 mins, mixing irregularly, 'til the vegetables are soft and the cheese is mildly overcooked.
5. Serve the grilled veggie and halloumi skewers as a main dish or with a side of pita bread or quinoa.

Per serving: Calories: 280 kcal; Fat: 18g; Carbs: 15g; Protein: 15g; Sodium: 600mg; Potassium: 400mg; Phosphorus: 300mg; Calcium: 400mg; Magnesium: 50mg

33. Baked Cod with Lemon-Herb Quinoa

Preparation time: fifteen mins

Cooking time: twenty mins

Servings: four

Ingredients:

- 4 cod fillets
- 1 lemon, juiced and zested
- two tbsps olive oil
- two pieces garlic, crushed
- one tbsp severed fresh dill
- one tsp dried parsley
- Salt and pepper as required
- one teacup quinoa
- two teacups vegetable broth
- two teacups steamed asparagus spears

Directions:

1. Warm up the oven to 400 deg. F.
2. Take the cod fillets in a baking dish. Spray with lemon juice and olive oil.
3. Spray crushed garlic, lemon zest, severed fresh dill, dried parsley, salt, and pepper over the cod fillets.
4. Bake the cod for 12-fifteen mins till it flakes simply with a fork.
5. During the baking process of the cod, prepare the quinoa by following the instructions on the package, substituting water with vegetable broth.
6. Serve the baked cod over lemon-herb quinoa with steamed asparagus spears on the side.

Per serving: Calories: 320 kcal; Fat: 10g; Carbs: 30g; Protein: 30g; Sodium: 400mg; Potassium: 600mg; Phosphorus: 300mg; Calcium: 80mg; Magnesium: 60mg

34. Vegetable Lentil Soup

Preparation time: fifteen mins

Cooking time: thirty mins

Servings: six

Ingredients:

- one tbsp olive oil
- one onion, severed
- two carrots, cubed
- 2 stalks celery, cubed
- two pieces garlic, crushed
- one teacup green lentils
- four teacups vegetable broth
- two teacups water
- one tin (14 oz) cubed tomatoes
- one tsp dried thyme
- one tsp dried rosemary
- Salt and pepper as required
- Chopped fresh parsley for garnish

Directions:

1. Inside a huge pot, temp. the olive oil across moderate flame. Include the severed onion, cubed carrots, cubed celery, and crushed garlic. Sauté till the vegetables are soft.
2. Include the green lentils, vegetable broth, water, cubed tomatoes (with their juice), dried thyme, dried rosemary, salt, and pepper to the pot. Stir thoroughly.
3. Boil the soup, afterwards diminish the temp. then simmer for 25-thirty mins 'til the lentils are cooked through and soft.
4. Season with additional salt & pepper if required. Garnish with severed fresh parsley prior to serving.

Per serving: Calories: 250 kcal; Fat: 3g; Carbs: 45g; Protein: 15g; Sodium: 500mg; Potassium: 800mg; Phosphorus: 250mg; Calcium: 60mg; Magnesium: 60mg

35. Spiced Up Pork Chops

Preparation time: four mins

Cooking time: fourteen mins

Servings: four

Ingredients:

- quarter teacup lime juice
- 1 mango (sliced)
- 4 pork rib chops
- two tsps cumin
- one tbsp coconut oil (dissolved)
- two garlic pieces (skinned and crushed)
- one tbsp chili powder

- one tsp ground cinnamon
- Salt and pepper as required
- half tsp hot pepper sauce

Directions:

1. Stir simultaneously lime juice, oil, garlic, cumin, cinnamon, chili powder, salt, pepper, and hot pepper sauce inside a blending container. Then put in the pork chops.
2. Put in the fridge for 4 hours if kept on the side. Warm up your grill to medium and place the pork chops on it. Give 7 minutes for every end on the grill.
3. Serve with mango pieces, divided amongst serving dishes.

Per serving: Calories: 400kcal; Carbs: 3g; Protein: 35g; Fat: 8g; Sodium: 136mg; Potassium: 572mg; Phosphorus: 224mg; Calcium: 29mg; Magnesium: 46mg

36. Baked Salmon with Quinoa and Roasted Vegetables

Preparation time: ten mins

Cooking time: twenty-five mins

Servings: four

Ingredients:

- 4 salmon fillets
- two teacups mixed vegetables (such as carrots, bell peppers, & broccoli)
- one teacup quinoa
- two tbsps olive oil
- Salt and pepper as required
- Lemon wedges for serving

Directions:

1. Warm up the oven to 400 deg. F.
2. Cook quinoa as per to the package directions.
3. Mix olive oil, salt, and pepper with the mixed veggies. Disperse them on a baking tray then roast for fifteen mins.
4. Season the salmon fillets with salt & pepper. Place them on another baking tray and bake for twelve-fifteen mins till cooked through.
5. Serve the salmon over cooked quinoa with roasted vegetables on the side.

Squeeze fresh lemon juice over the salmon prior to serving.

Per serving: Calories: 350 kcal; Fat: 15g; Carbs: 20g; Protein: 30g; Sodium: 100mg; Potassium: 600mg; Phosphorus: 350mg; Calcium: 50mg; Magnesium: 70mg

37. Salmon with Quinoa and Steamed Broccoli

Preparation time: ten mins

Cooking time: twenty mins

Servings: four

Ingredients:

- 4 salmon fillets
- one teacup quinoa
- two teacups vegetable broth
- one tbsp olive oil
- two pieces garlic, crushed
- one tsp dried dill
- one tsp lemon zest
- one tbsp lemon juice
- Salt and pepper as required
- two teacups steamed broccoli florets

Directions:

1. Warm up the oven to 400 deg. F.
2. Cook quinoa as per to the package directions, utilizing vegetable broth instead of water.
3. In your small container, blend the crushed garlic, dried dill, lemon zest, lemon juice, salt, and pepper.
4. Arrange the salmon fillets on a baking tray and proceed to spray them with olive oil. Next, generously spray the garlic-dill solution over the fillets to season them.
5. Bake the salmon for 12-fifteen mins 'til cooked through and flaky.
6. Serve the baked salmon over cooked quinoa with steamed broccoli on the side.

Per serving: Calories: 380 kcal; Fat: 15g; Carbs: 30g; Protein: 30g; Sodium: 300mg; Potassium: 800mg; Phosphorus: 300mg; Calcium: 80mg; Magnesium: 70mg

38. Pork and Sweet Potatoes

Preparation time: ten mins

Cooking time: one hr and twenty mins

Servings: 8

Ingredients:

- 2 pounds sweet potatoes, severed
- A spray of olive oil
- one yellow onion, severed
- 2 pounds pork meat, ground
- one tbsp chili powder
- Black pepper as required
- one tsp cumin, ground
- half tsp garlic powder
- half tsp oregano, severed
- half tsp cinnamon powder
- one teacup low-sodium veggie stock
- half teacup cilantro, severed

Directions:

1. Warm a pot with the oil over moderate-high flame, include sweet potatoes and onion, stir, cook for fifteen mins and transfer to a container.

2. Warm the pot again over moderate-high flame, include pork, stir and brown for five mins. Include black pepper, cumin, garlic powder, oregano, chili powder, and cinnamon, stock, return potatoes and onion, stir and cook for one hr across moderate flame.

3. Include the cilantro, toss, split into containers and serve.

Per serving: Calories: 296kcal; Carbs: 26g; Protein: 11g; Fat: 8g; Sodium: 209mg; Potassium: 600mg; Phosphorus: 400mg; Calcium: 60mg; Magnesium: 40mg

39. Turkey and Vegetable Stir-Fry

Preparation time: ten mins

Cooking time: fifteen mins

Servings: four

Ingredients:

- 1 lb. ground turkey
- two teacups mixed vegetables (like snap peas, bell peppers, and carrots), sliced
- one tbsp sesame oil
- two tbsps low-sodium soy sauce
- two pieces garlic, crushed
- one tsp grated ginger
- quarter tsp red pepper flakes (optional)
- Salt and pepper as required
- Chopped green onions for garnish

Directions:

1. Place a griddle/wok on moderate-high flame and warm the sesame oil.

2. Include the ground turkey then cook till browned, breaking it up with a spoon.

3. Include the crushed garlic, grated ginger, and red pepper flakes (if utilizing). Stir-fry for one min.

4. Include the mixed vegetables and cook for three-four mins till they are soft-crisp.

5. Stir in the low-sodium soy sauce and season with salt and pepper.

6. Garnish with severed green onions prior to serving. Serve over brown rice/quinoa if anticipated.

Per serving: Calories: 280 kcal; Fat: 10gm; Carbs: 15g; Protein: 30g; Sodium: 400mg; Potassium: 500mg; Phosphorus: 300mg; Calcium: 40mg; Magnesium: 40mg

40. Pork with Dates Sauce

Preparation time: ten mins

Cooking time: forty mins

Servings: six

Ingredients:

- one and half-pounds pork tenderloin
- two tbsps water
- one-third teacup dates, eroded
- quarter tsp onion powder
- quarter tsp smoked paprika
- two tbsps mustard
- quarter teacup coconut amino
- Black pepper as required

Directions:

1. Pulse the dates, water, coconut amino, mustard, paprika, pepper, and onion powder in the container you use for processing. Pulse until the dates are completely smooth.

2. Put pork tenderloin in a roasting pot, include the dates sauce, toss to coat very well, introduce everything in the oven at 400°F, bake for forty mins, slice the meat, split it and the sauce between plates and serve.

Per serving: Calories: 332kcal; Carbs: 50g; Protein: 7.4g; Fat: 13.7g; Sodium: 226mg; Potassium: 419mg; Phosphorus: 376mg; Calcium: 30mg; Magnesium: 38mg

41. Grilled Chicken with Roasted Sweet Potatoes and Green Beans

Preparation time: fifteen mins

Cooking time: twenty-five mins

Servings: four

Ingredients:

- four boneless, skinless chicken breasts
- two average sweet potatoes, skinned and cubed
- one lb. green beans, trimmed
- two tbsps olive oil
- one tsp smoked paprika
- half tsp garlic powder
- Salt and pepper as required

Directions:

1. Warm up the grill to moderate-high flame.
2. Add salt, pepper, smoked paprika, and garlic powder to the chicken breasts.
3. Combine the cubed sweet potatoes and green beans inside a big container, and coat them with olive oil, salt, and pepper.
4. Cook the chicken on the grill, flipping it after 6-eight mins on every end, till it is fully cooked.
5. Arrange the sweet potatoes and green beans on a baking tray, then roast them in the oven at 400 deg. F for 15-twenty mins, or till they become soft.
6. Serve the grilled chicken with roasted sweet potatoes and green beans on the side.

Per serving: Calories: 320 kcal; Fat: 10g; Carbs: 25g; Protein: 30g; Sodium: 150mg;

Potassium: 800mg; Phosphorus: 350mg; Calcium: 70mg; Magnesium: 70mg

42. Baked Cod with Quinoa and Steamed Asparagus

Preparation time: ten mins

Cooking time: twenty mins

Servings: four

Ingredients:

- 4 cod fillets
- one teacup quinoa
- 1 bunch asparagus, trimmed
- two tbsps olive oil
- two pieces garlic, crushed
- one tsp lemon zest
- one tbsp lemon juice
- Salt and pepper as required

Directions:

1. Warm up the oven to 400 deg. F.
2. Cook quinoa as per to the package directions.
3. Arrange the cod fillets onto a baking tray. Spray them with olive oil then spray them with salt, pepper, crushed garlic, lemon zest, and lemon juice.
4. Bake the cod fillets for 12-fifteen mins till cooked through and flaky.
5. Meanwhile, steam the asparagus till soft, about five mins.
6. Serve the baked cod over cooked quinoa with steamed asparagus on the side.

Per serving: Calories: 250 kcal; Fat: 8g; Carbs: 20g; Protein: 25g; Sodium: 150mg; Potassium: 600mg; Phosphorus: 300mg; Calcium: 60mg; Magnesium: 60mg

43. Lentil and Vegetable Curry

Preparation time: fifteen mins

Cooking time: thirty mins

Servings: 6

Ingredients:

- one teacup dried lentils, washed
- one tbsp olive oil
- one onion, severed

- two pieces garlic, crushed
- one tbsp curry powder
- one tsp ground cumin
- half tsp ground turmeric
- quarter tsp cayenne pepper (optional)
- two teacups severed vegetables (like bell peppers, carrots, and zucchini)
- one tin (fourteen oz) cubed tomatoes
- one tin (fourteen oz) coconut milk
- Salt and pepper as required
- Chopped fresh cilantro for garnish

Directions:

1. Cook the lentils as per to the package directions. Drain and put away.
2. Inside a huge saucepot, warm the olive oil across moderate flame. Include the onion & garlic then sauté till softened.
3. Include the curry powder, cumin, turmeric, and cayenne pepper (if utilizing). Cook for 1 minute till fragrant.
4. Include the severed vegetables, cubed tomatoes, and cooked lentils to the saucepot. Stir thoroughly.
5. Pour in the coconut milk, afterwards raise the solution to a simmer. Cook for 15-twenty mins, 'til the vegetables are soft.
6. Season with salt and pepper as required. Garnish with severed fresh cilantro prior to serving.

Per serving: Calories: 270 kcal; Fat: 12g; Carbs: 30g; Protein: 10g; Sodium: 300mg; Potassium: 600mg; Phosphorus: 150mg; Calcium: 80mg; Magnesium: 50mg

44. Chicken Stir-Fry with Brown Rice

Preparation time: fifteen mins

Cooking time: fifteen mins

Servings: four

Ingredients:

- 2 boneless, skinless chicken breasts, sliced
- two tbsps low-sodium soy sauce
- one tbsp cornstarch
- one tbsp olive oil

- two pieces garlic, crushed
- one tbsp grated fresh ginger
- one red bell pepper, sliced
- one yellow bell pepper, sliced
- one teacup broccoli florets
- one teacup snap peas
- 1 carrot, julienned
- quarter teacup low-sodium chicken broth
- two tbsps hoisin sauce
- Cooked brown rice for serving

Directions:

1. Inside your container, blend sliced chicken breasts, low-sodium soy sauce, and cornstarch. Toss to coat the chicken uniformly.
2. Warm olive oil inside a big griddle or wok over moderate-high flame. Include crushed garlic and grated fresh ginger, and cook for one min till fragrant.
3. Include the chicken to the griddle then stir-fry for 5-six mins till cooked through.
4. Include sliced red bell pepper, sliced yellow bell pepper, broccoli florets, snap peas, and julienned carrot to the griddle. Stir-fry for 3-four mins 'til the vegetables are crisp-soft.
5. In your small container, whisk simultaneously low-sodium chicken broth and hoisin sauce. Pour the sauce across the chicken & vegetables, then cook for an extra one to two mins 'til heated through.
6. Serve the chicken stir-fry over cooked brown rice.

Per serving: Calories: 320 kcal; Fat: 6g; Carbs: 40g; Protein: 25g; Sodium: 600mg; Potassium: 600mg; Phosphorus: 300mg; Calcium: 60mg; Magnesium: 70mg

45. Herbed Butter Pork Chops

Preparation time: ten mins

Cooking time: twenty-five mins

Servings: two

Ingredients:

- one tbsp almond butter (divided)
- 2 boneless pork chops
- one tbsp olive oil
- Salt and pepper as required
- one tbsp dried
- Italian seasoning as required

Directions:

1. Warm up the oven to 350 deg. F. Take out the pork chops from the pot and dry them with a paper towel.
2. After that, put them on a baking dish. Include salt, pepper, and Italian seasoning as per taste. Spray olive oil over pork chops and smear half tablespoon of butter on each chop. Warm up the oven to about 350 deg. F and bake for twenty-five mins.
3. Place the pork chops on two plates and spray with the butter juice. Serve.

Per serving: Calories: 333kcal; Carbs: 1g; Protein: 31g; Fat: 23g; Sodium: 242mg; Potassium: 370mg; Phosphorus: 206mg; Calcium: 33mg; Magnesium: 53mg

CHAPTER 4

SNACKS AND APPETIZERS

46. Quinoa Salad Cups   38

47. Avocado Hummus   38

48. Tuna Stuffed Cucumber Bites   38

49. Smashed Chickpea Salad Wraps   38

50. Tuna Cucumber Bites   39

51. Cucumber and Hummus Roll-Ups   39

52. Greek Salad Skewers   39

53. Caprese Skewers   40

54. Mango Salsa   40

55. Roasted Red Pepper Hummus   40

56. Greek Cucumber Cups   41

57. Quinoa and Black Bean Salad Cups   41

58. Oven-Baked Zucchini Chips   41

59. Greek Yogurt and Fruit Parfait   42

60. Yogurt-Dipped Strawberries   42

46. Quinoa Salad Cups

Preparation time: twenty mins

Cooking time: fifteen mins

Servings: 12

Ingredients:

- one teacup cooked quinoa
- one teacup cubed cucumber
- one teacup cubed tomatoes
- quarter teacup severed fresh parsley
- two tbsps lemon juice
- two tbsps olive oil
- Salt and pepper, as required
- 12 lettuce cups (such as butter or romaine)

Directions:

1. Inside your container, blend cooked quinoa, cucumber, tomatoes, parsley, lemon juice, olive oil, salt, & pepper.
2. Mix thoroughly 'til all components are uniformly coated.
3. Spoon the quinoa salad into lettuce cups.
4. Serve chilled.

Per serving: Calories: 68 kcal; Fat: 4g; Carbs: 7gm; Protein: 2gm; Sodium: 7mg; Potassium: 120mg; Phosphorus: 38mg; Calcium: 10mg; Magnesium: 16mg

47. Avocado Hummus

Preparation time: ten mins

Cooking time: zero mins

Servings: 6

Ingredients:

- one ripe avocado, skinned and eroded
- one tin (15 ounces) chickpeas, drained and washed
- two pieces garlic, crushed
- two tbsps fresh lemon juice
- two tbsps olive oil
- quarter tsp salt
- quarter tsp ground cumin
- quarter tsp paprika
- Fresh cilantro, for garnish

Directions:

1. Inside a blending container, blend avocado, chickpeas, garlic, lemon juice, olive oil, salt, cumin, and paprika.
2. Blend till level and creamy.
3. Bring to a serving container then garnish with fresh cilantro.
4. Serve with fresh vegetables or whole-grain pita bread.

Per serving: Calories: 152 kcal; Fat: 8g; Carbs: 16g; Protein: 5g; Sodium: 207mg; Potassium: 296mg; Phosphorus: 86mg; Calcium: 32mg; Magnesium: 27mg

48. Tuna Stuffed Cucumber Bites

Preparation time: fifteen mins

Cooking time: zero mins

Servings: four

Ingredients:

- one big cucumber
- one tin (5 ounces) tuna, drained
- two tbsps Greek yogurt
- one tbsp severed red onion
- one tbsp severed celery
- one tbsp severed fresh dill
- Salt and pepper, as required

Directions:

1. Cut the cucumber into one-inch dense slices.
2. Using a spoon/melon baller, hollow out the centers of the cucumber slices to create a small well.
3. Inside your container, mix simultaneously tuna, Greek yogurt, red onion, celery, dill, salt, and pepper.
4. Spoon the tuna solution into the cucumber wells.
5. Serve chilled.

Per serving: Calories: 97 kcal; Fat: 2g; Carbs: 5g; Protein: 15g; Sodium: 189mg; Potassium: 284mg; Phosphorus: 131mg; Calcium: 31mg; Magnesium: 22mg

49. Smashed Chickpea Salad Wraps

Preparation time: fifteen mins

Cooking time: zero mins

Servings: four

Ingredients:

- one tin (fifteen oz.) chickpeas, drained and washed
- quarter teacup cubed red onion
- quarter teacup cubed celery
- quarter teacup cubed bell pepper
- two tbsps severed fresh parsley
- two tbsps Greek yogurt
- one tbsp lemon juice
- one tbsp olive oil
- half tsp Dijon mustard
- Salt and pepper, as required
- 4 whole-wtemp. tortillas
- Lettuce leaves, for serving

Directions:

1. Inside your container, use a fork to mash the chickpeas till they are partially smashed.
2. Include red onion, celery, bell pepper, parsley, Greek yogurt, lemon juice, olive oil, Dijon mustard, salt, and pepper to the container. Mix thoroughly.
3. Warm the tortillas in a dry griddle or microwave.
4. Place a lettuce leaf on each tortilla then spoon the chickpea salad over the lettuce.
5. Roll up the tortillas tightly to form wraps.
6. Cut the wraps in half and serve.

Per serving: Calories: 198 kcal; Fat: 7g; Carbs: 27g; Protein: 7g; Sodium: 230mg; Potassium: 295mg; Phosphorus: 90mg; Calcium: 71mg; Magnesium: 41mg

50. Tuna Cucumber Bites

Preparation time: ten mins

Cooking time: zero mins

Servings: four

Ingredients:

- one big cucumber
- one tin (5 ounces) tuna, drained

- two tbsps Greek yogurt
- one tbsp lemon juice
- one tbsp severed fresh dill
- Salt and pepper, as required

Directions:

1. Cut the cucumber into thick slices.
2. Inside your container, blend drained tuna, Greek yogurt, lemon juice, severed dill, salt, and pepper. Mix thoroughly.
3. Spoon a small amount of the tuna solution onto each cucumber slice.
4. Serve chilled.

Per serving: Calories: 73 kcal; Fat: 1g; Carbs: 3g; Protein: 13g; Sodium: 183mg; Potassium: 196mg; Phosphorus: 129mg; Calcium: 17mg; Magnesium: 13mg

51. Cucumber and Hummus Roll-Ups

Preparation time: ten mins

Cooking time: zero mins

Servings: four

Ingredients:

- one big cucumber
- half teacup hummus
- two tbsps severed fresh parsley

Directions:

1. Cut the cucumber lengthwise into thin strips utilizing a vegetable peeler or a mandoline slicer.
2. Apply a thin coating of hummus onto every cucumber strip.
3. Spray severed parsley over the hummus.
4. If you need to, you can use toothpicks to hold the cucumber strips together.
5. Serve chilled.

Per serving: Calories: 64 kcal; Fat: 3g; Carbs: 7g; Protein: 3g; Sodium: 133mg; Potassium: 214mg; Phosphorus: 46mg; Calcium: 22mg; Magnesium: 15mg

52. Greek Salad Skewers

Preparation time: fifteen mins

Cooking time: zero mins

Servings: four

Ingredients:

- one cucumber, cut into chunks
- one teacup cherry tomatoes
- one teacup cubed feta cheese
- quarter teacup pitted Kalamata olives
- two tbsps olive oil
- one tbsp fresh lemon juice
- one tbsp severed fresh oregano
- Salt and pepper, as required
- 4 skewers

Directions:

1. Alternate the pieces of cucumber, cherry tomatoes, feta cheese, and Kalamata olives as you thread them onto the skewers.
2. In your small container, whisk simultaneously olive oil, lemon juice, oregano, salt, and pepper.
3. Spray the dressing across the skewers.
4. Serve chilled.

Per serving: Calories: 203 kcal; Fat: 18g; Carbs: 5g; Protein: 6g; Sodium: 480mg; Potassium: 150mg; Phosphorus: 125mg; Calcium: 180mg; Magnesium: 13mg

53. Caprese Skewers

Preparation time: ten mins

Cooking time: zero mins

Servings: four

Ingredients:

- 1 pint cherry tomatoes
- sixteen small fresh mozzarella balls
- sixteen fresh basil leaves
- two tbsps balsamic glaze
- Salt and pepper, as required
- 4 skewers

Directions:

1. Thread a cherry tomato, fresh mozzarella ball, and basil leaf onto each skewer, repeating till all components are used.
2. Arrange the skewers on a serving platter.
3. Spray balsamic glaze over the skewers and season with salt and pepper.

4. Serve instantly.

Per serving: Calories: 117 kcal; Fat: 8g; Carbs: 4g; Protein: 8g; Sodium: 50mg; Potassium: 133mg; Phosphorus: 118mg; Calcium: 179mg; Magnesium: 11mg

54. Mango Salsa

Preparation time: ten mins

Cooking time: zero mins

Servings: 6

Ingredients:

- 2 ripe mangoes, skinned and cubed
- half teacup cubed red bell pepper
- quarter teacup severed red onion
- quarter teacup severed fresh cilantro
- Juice of one lime
- Salt and pepper, as required

Directions:

1. Inside your container, blend cubed mangoes, red bell pepper, red onion, cilantro, lime juice, salt, and pepper.
2. Mix thoroughly to blend the entire components.
3. Chill for around thirty mins to allow the flavors to blend simultaneously.
4. Serve chilled with whole-grain tortilla chips or as a topping for grilled chicken or fish.

Per serving: Calories: 61 kcal; Fat: 0g; Carbs: 16g; Protein: 1g; Sodium: 2mg; Potassium: 194mg; Phosphorus: 14mg; Calcium: 11mg; Magnesium: 9mg

55. Roasted Red Pepper Hummus

Preparation time: ten mins

Cooking time: twenty-five mins

Servings: 6

Ingredients:

- one tin (fifteen oz.) chickpeas, drained and washed
- one roasted red pepper, skinned and sowed
- two tbsps tahini
- two tbsps lemon juice
- 1 clove garlic

- two tbsps olive oil
- half tsp cumin
- Salt and pepper, as required

Directions:

1. Warm up the oven to 425 deg. F.
2. Place the roasted red pepper on a baking tray and roast for 20-twenty-five mins, or 'til the skin is charred.
3. Eliminate the pepper from the oven then let it cool. Once cooled, peel off the skin then remove the seeds.
4. In your blending container, blend chickpeas, roasted red pepper, tahini, lemon juice, garlic, olive oil, cumin, salt, and pepper.
5. Process till level and creamy.
6. Transfer the hummus to a serving container.
7. Serve with sliced vegetables or whole-grain crackers.

Per serving: Calories: 120 kcal; Fat: 7g; Carbs: 11g; Protein: 4g; Sodium: 152mg; Potassium: 119mg; Phosphorus: 70mg; Calcium: 23mg; Magnesium: 19mg

56. Greek Cucumber Cups

Preparation time: fifteen mins

Cooking time: zero mins

Servings: four

Ingredients:

- two big cucumbers
- one teacup cubed tomatoes
- half teacup crumbled feta cheese
- two tbsps severed fresh dill
- two tbsps lemon juice
- one tbsp olive oil
- Salt and pepper, as required

Directions:

1. Cut the cucumbers into one-inch thick slices.
2. Use a melon baller/spoon to scoop out the centers of the cucumber slices, creating a cup shape.

3. Inside your container, blend cubed tomatoes, feta cheese, olive oil, dill, lemon juice, salt, & pepper.
4. Spoon the tomato solution into the cucumber cups.
5. Serve chilled.

Per serving: Calories: 76 kcal; Fat: 5gm; Carbs: 6g; Protein: 3g; Sodium: 170mg; Potassium: 223mg; Phosphorus: 67mg; Calcium: 92mg; Magnesium: 16mg

57. Quinoa and Black Bean Salad Cups

Preparation time: fifteen mins

Cooking time: zero mins

Servings: four

Ingredients:

- one teacup cooked quinoa
- one teacup canned black beans, washed & drained
- half teacup cubed red bell pepper
- half teacup cubed cucumber
- quarter teacup cubed red onion
- two tbsps severed fresh cilantro
- two tbsps lime juice
- one tbsp olive oil
- Salt and pepper, as required
- Lettuce leaves, for serving

Directions:

1. Inside your container, blend cooked quinoa, black beans, red bell pepper, cucumber, red onion, cilantro, lime juice, olive oil, salt, and pepper. Mix thoroughly.
2. Spoon the quinoa and black bean salad into lettuce leaves, creating cups.
3. Serve chilled.

Per serving: Calories: 159 kcal; Fat: 4g; Carbs: 25g; Protein: 7gm; Sodium: 11mg; Potassium: 365mg; Phosphorus: 123mg; Calcium: 34mg; Magnesium: 53mg

58. Oven-Baked Zucchini Chips

Preparation time: ten mins

Cooking time: twenty-five mins

Servings: four

Ingredients:

- two average zucchinis, sliced into thin rounds
- two tbsps grated Parmesan cheese
- one tbsp olive oil
- half tsp garlic powder
- half tsp dried oregano
- Salt and pepper, as required

Directions:

1. Warm up the oven to 425 deg. F.
2. Inside your container, toss zucchini rounds with Parmesan cheese, olive oil, garlic powder, dried oregano, salt, and pepper.
3. Place the zucchini rounds uniformly on a baking tray in a single layer.
4. Bake for 20-twenty-five mins, flipping halfway through, 'til the chips are crispy and golden.
5. Serve warm or at room temp.

Per serving: Calories: 57 kcal; Fat: 4g; Carbs: 4g; Protein: 2g; Sodium: 88mg; Potassium: 299mg; Phosphorus: 37mg; Calcium: 54mg; Magnesium: 25mg

59. Greek Yogurt and Fruit Parfait

Preparation time: ten mins

Cooking time: zero mins

Servings: one

Ingredients:

- half teacup non-fat Greek yogurt
- quarter teacup granola
- quarter teacup mixed fresh berries (such as strawberries, blueberries, and raspberries)
- one tbsp honey (optional)

Directions:

1. In your glass or container, layer half of the Greek yogurt, granola, and mixed berries.
2. Repeat the layers with the remaining components.
3. Spray honey over the top, if anticipated.
4. Serve instantly.

Per serving: Calories: 186 kcal; Fat: 3g; Carbs: 32g; Protein: 13g; Sodium: 59mg; Potassium: 180mg; Phosphorus: 171mg; Calcium: 142mg; Magnesium: 15mg

60. Yogurt-Dipped Strawberries

Preparation time: ten mins

Cooking time: zero mins

Servings: four

Ingredients:

- one teacup non-fat Greek yogurt
- one tbsp honey
- one tsp vanilla extract
- 16 fresh strawberries

Directions:

1. Inside your container, mix simultaneously Greek yogurt, honey, and vanilla extract till well combined.
2. Dip each strawberry into the yogurt solution, coating it halfway.
3. Place the dipped strawberries on a plate lined with parchment paper.
4. Take the plate in the freezer for about thirty mins, or till the yogurt is set.
5. Serve chilled.

Per serving: Calories: 73 kcal; Fat: 0g; Carbs: 15g; Protein: 5g; Sodium: 20mg; Potassium: 236mg; Phosphorus: 55mg; Calcium: 63mg; Magnesium: 17mg

CHAPTER 5
SIDE DISHES

61. CAPRESE SKEWERS WITH BALSAMIC GLAZE   44

62. BROWN RICE PILAF WITH VEGETABLES   44

63. STEAMED ASPARAGUS WITH LEMON GARLIC SAUCE   44

64. SPINACH AND MUSHROOM QUICHE   45

65. CUCUMBER AND TOMATO SALAD   45

66. QUINOA AND VEGETABLE SALAD   45

67. STEAMED ASPARAGUS WITH LEMON BUTTER SAUCE   46

68. ROASTED BEET AND ARUGULA SALAD   46

69. CUCUMBER AND WATERMELON SALAD   46

70. OVEN-ROASTED GREEN BEANS   47

71. ROASTED BRUSSELS SPROUTS WITH BALSAMIC GLAZE 47

72. LEMON GARLIC ROASTED ZUCCHINI   47

73. STEAMED BROCCOLI WITH LEMON GARLIC SAUCE   47

74. STEAMED EDAMAME WITH SEA SALT   48

75. GRILLED EGGPLANT WITH BALSAMIC GLAZE   48

61. Caprese Skewers with Balsamic Glaze

Preparation time: fifteen mins

Cooking time: zero mins

Servings: four

Ingredients:

- 1 pint cherry tomatoes
- 8 small fresh mozzarella balls
- Fresh basil leaves
- Balsamic glaze for drizzling
- Salt and pepper as required

Directions:

1. On skewers, alternate threading cherry tomatoes, fresh mozzarella balls, and basil leaves.
2. Arrange the skewers on a serving platter.
3. Spray with balsamic glaze.
4. Spray with salt and pepper.
5. Serve chilled.

Per serving: Calories: 140 kcal; Fat: 9gm; Carbs: 5g; Protein: 9g; Sodium: 200mg; Potassium: 190mg; Phosphorus: 160mg; Calcium: 180mg; Magnesium: 20mg

62. Brown Rice Pilaf with Vegetables

Preparation time: ten mins

Cooking time: thirty mins

Servings: four

Ingredients:

- one teacup brown rice
- two teacups low-sodium vegetable broth
- one tbsp olive oil
- one small onion, finely severed
- 1 carrot, cubed
- one red bell pepper, cubed
- one zucchini, cubed
- two pieces garlic, crushed
- one tsp dried thyme
- Salt and pepper as required

Directions:

1. Wash the brown rice under cold water.
2. In your saucepot, raise the vegetable broth to a boil.
3. Include the washed brown rice to the boiling broth, diminish the temp., cover, then simmer for twenty to twenty-five mins 'til the rice is soft and the liquid is engrossed.
4. In a different griddle, temp. olive oil across moderate flame.
5. Sauté the onion, carrot, red bell pepper, zucchini, garlic, dried thyme, salt, and pepper till the vegetables are soft.
6. Stir the sautéed vegetables into the cooked brown rice.
7. Fluff with a fork and serve.

Per serving: Calories: 180 kcal; Fat: 4g; Carbs: 33g; Protein: 4g; Sodium: 240mg; Potassium: 290mg; Phosphorus: 100mg; Calcium: 40mg; Magnesium: 60mg

63. Steamed Asparagus with Lemon Garlic Sauce

Preparation time: ten mins

Cooking time: ten mins

Servings: four

Ingredients:

- 1 bunch asparagus
- two tbsps olive oil
- two pieces garlic, crushed
- Juice of one lemon
- Salt and pepper as required

Directions:

1. Trim the tough ends of the asparagus.
2. Steam the asparagus till crisp-soft, about five to seven mins.
3. In your small pot, temp. olive oil across moderate flame and sauté the crushed garlic till fragrant.
4. Take the pot from temp. then stir in lemon juice, salt, and pepper.
5. Drizzle the lemon garlic sauce over the steamed asparagus prior to serving.

Per serving: Calories: 80 kcal; Fat: 7g; Carbs: 4g; Protein: 2g; Sodium: 5mg; Potassium: 220mg; Phosphorus: 50mg; Calcium: 30mg; Magnesium: 20mg

64. Spinach and Mushroom Quiche

Preparation time: fifteen mins

Cooking time: forty mins

Servings: four

Ingredients:

- 1 pre-made pie crust
- one teacup fresh spinach, severed
- one teacup mushrooms, sliced
- 4 big eggs
- one teacup skim milk
- half teacup shredded low-fat cheddar cheese
- Salt and pepper as required

Directions:

1. Warm up the oven to 375 deg. F.
2. Bring the pie crust inside a pie dish then put away.
3. In a griddle, sauté the spinach and mushrooms 'til the spinach is wilted and the mushrooms are soft.
4. Inside your container, whisk simultaneously eggs, milk, salt, and pepper.
5. Disperse the sautéed spinach and mushrooms uniformly over the pie crust.
6. Pour the egg solution over the vegetables.
7. Spray shredded cheddar cheese on top.
8. Bake for 35-forty mins 'til the quiche is set and golden brown.
9. Allow to cool mildly prior to serving.

Per serving: Calories: 250 kcal; Fat: 12g; Carbs: 21g; Protein: 15g; Sodium: 340mg; Potassium: 400mg; Phosphorus: 250mg; Calcium: 250mg; Magnesium: 45mg

65. Cucumber and Tomato Salad

Preparation time: ten mins

Cooking time: zero mins

Servings: four

Ingredients:

- 2 cucumbers, skinned and sliced
- 2 tomatoes, cubed
- one small red onion, finely sliced
- two tbsps fresh lemon juice
- two tbsps olive oil
- one tbsp severed fresh dill
- Salt and pepper as required

Directions:

1. Inside a huge container, blend cucumbers, tomatoes, and red onion.
2. Inside a different small container, whisk simultaneously lemon juice, olive oil, dill, salt, & pepper to make the dressing.
3. Pour the dressing over the cucumber & tomato solution.
4. Toss gently to coat.
5. Put in the fridge for thirty mins prior to serving.

Per serving: Calories: 90 kcal; Fat: 6g; Carbs: 9g; Protein: 2g; Sodium: 15mg; Potassium: 360mg; Phosphorus: 35mg; Calcium: 30mg; Magnesium: 30mg

66. Quinoa and Vegetable Salad

Preparation time: fifteen mins

Cooking time: fifteen mins

Servings: four

Ingredients:

- one teacup quinoa
- two teacups low-sodium vegetable broth
- one red bell pepper, cubed
- one cucumber, cubed
- half teacup cherry tomatoes, shared
- quarter teacup severed fresh parsley
- two tbsps olive oil
- two tbsps lemon juice
- Salt and pepper as required

Directions:

1. Wash the quinoa under cold water.
2. In your saucepot, raise the vegetable broth to a boil.
3. Include the washed quinoa to the boiling broth, diminish the temp., cover, then simmer for twelve-fifteen mins 'til the quinoa is cooked and the liquid is absorbed.

4. Inside a huge container, blend the cooked quinoa, cubed red bell pepper, cubed cucumber, shared cherry tomatoes, severed fresh parsley, olive oil, lemon juice, salt, and pepper.

5. Toss gently to blend.

6. Serve chilled.

Per serving: Calories: 220 kcal; Fat: 8gm; Carbs: 32gm; Protein: 6g; Sodium: 10mg; Potassium: 460mg; Phosphorus: 160mg; Calcium: 30mg; Magnesium: 85mg

67. Steamed Asparagus with Lemon Butter Sauce

Preparation time: ten mins

Cooking time: ten mins

Servings: four

Ingredients:

- 1 bunch asparagus, ends trimmed
- two tbsps unsalted butter
- Zest and juice of one lemon
- Salt and pepper as required

Directions:

1. Steam the asparagus till soft-crisp, around five to seven mins.

2. Inside your small saucepot, dissolve the butter across low temp.

3. Take the saucepan from temp. then stir in the lemon zest, lemon juice, salt, & pepper.

4. Drizzle the lemon butter sauce over the steamed asparagus prior to serving.

Per serving: Calories: 80 kcal; Fat: 6g; Carbs: 5gm; Protein: 3g; Sodium: 5mg; Potassium: 230mg; Phosphorus: 60mg; Calcium: 30mg; Magnesium: 20mg

68. Roasted Beet and Arugula Salad

Preparation time: fifteen mins

Cooking time: forty-five mins

Servings: four

Ingredients:

- 4 medium beets, skinned and cubed
- two tbsps olive oil
- Salt and pepper as required
- four teacups arugula
- quarter teacup crumbled goat cheese
- quarter teacup severed walnuts
- two tbsps balsamic vinegar

Directions:

1. Warm up the oven to 400 deg. F.

2. Mix the beet cubes with the salt and pepper and the olive oil.

3. Disperse the seasoned beets on a baking tray in a single layer.

4. Roast for 40-forty-five mins till the beets are soft.

5. Inside a huge salad container, blend the roasted beets, arugula, crumbled goat cheese, severed walnuts, and balsamic vinegar.

6. Toss gently to blend.

7. Serve chilled.

Per serving: Calories: 160 kcal; Fat: 12g; Carbs: 10g; Protein: 5g; Sodium: 150mg; Potassium: 500mg; Phosphorus: 80mg; Calcium: 50mg; Magnesium: 35mg

69. Cucumber and Watermelon Salad

Preparation time: ten mins

Cooking time: zero mins

Servings: four

Ingredients:

- two teacups cubed watermelon
- 1 English cucumber, sliced
- quarter teacup crumbled feta cheese
- two tbsps severed fresh mint
- one tbsp lime juice
- Salt and pepper as required

Directions:

1. Inside a huge container, blend cubed watermelon, sliced cucumber, crumbled feta cheese, severed fresh mint, lime juice, salt, and pepper.

2. Toss gently to blend.

3. Serve chilled.

Per serving: Calories: 60 kcal; Fat: 2gm; Carbs: 10g; Protein: 2g; Sodium: 120mg;

Potassium: 220mg; Phosphorus: 45mg; Calcium: 50mg; Magnesium: 15mg

70. Oven-Roasted Green Beans

Preparation time: ten mins

Cooking time: fifteen mins

Servings: four

Ingredients:

- one lb. fresh green beans, trimmed
- two tbsps olive oil
- two pieces garlic, crushed
- Salt and pepper as required
- Grated Parmesan cheese for topping

Directions:

1. Warm up the oven to 425 deg. F.
2. Toss the green beans with crushed garlic, olive oil, salt, and pepper.
3. Arrange the green beans on a baking tray, ensuring they are spread out uniformly.
4. Roast for 12-fifteen mins till the green beans are crisp-soft and mildly charred.
5. Spray with grated Parmesan cheese prior to serving.

Per serving: Calories: 90 kcal; Fat: 7g; Carbs: 7g; Protein: 2g; Sodium: 15mg; Potassium: 240mg; Phosphorus: 45mg; Calcium: 50mg; Magnesium: 25mg

71. Roasted Brussels Sprouts with Balsamic Glaze

Preparation time: ten mins

Cooking time: twenty-five mins

Servings: four

Ingredients:

- one lb. Brussels sprouts, trimmed and shared
- two tbsps olive oil
- Salt and pepper as required
- Balsamic glaze for drizzling

Directions:

1. Warm up the oven to 425 deg. F.
2. Coat the shared Brussels sprouts with olive oil, salt, and pepper.

3. Position the Brussels sprouts in a single layer on a baking tray.
4. Roast for twenty to twenty-five mins 'til the Brussels sprouts are soft and mildly browned.
5. Drizzle with balsamic glaze prior to serving.

Per serving: Calories: 90 kcal; Fat: 6g; Carbs: 8g; Protein: 3g; Sodium: 25mg; Potassium: 400mg; Phosphorus: 70mg; Calcium: 40mg; Magnesium: 25mg

72. Lemon Garlic Roasted Zucchini

Preparation time: ten mins

Cooking time: fifteen mins

Servings: four

Ingredients:

- two average zucchini, sliced into rounds
- two tbsps olive oil
- two pieces garlic, crushed
- Zest and juice of one lemon
- Salt and pepper as required
- Chopped fresh parsley for garnish

Directions:

1. Warm up the oven to 425 deg. F.
2. Inside a huge container, toss the zucchini rounds with olive oil, crushed garlic, lemon zest, lemon juice, salt, and pepper.
3. Disperse the seasoned zucchini on a baking tray in a single layer.
4. Roast for 12-fifteen mins till the zucchini is soft and mildly browned.
5. Garnish with severed fresh parsley prior to serving.

Per serving: Calories: 80 kcal; Fat: 7g; Carbs: 4g; Protein: 1g; Sodium: 5mg; Potassium: 270mg; Phosphorus: 30mg; Calcium: 20mg; Magnesium: 20mg

73. Steamed Broccoli with Lemon Garlic Sauce

Preparation time: ten mins

Cooking time: ten mins

Servings: four

Ingredients:

- 2 heads broccoli, cut into florets
- two tbsps olive oil
- two pieces garlic, crushed
- Juice of 1 lemon
- Salt and pepper as required

Directions:

1. Steam the broccoli florets till crisp-soft, around five to seven mins.
2. In your small pot, temp. olive oil across moderate flame and sauté the crushed garlic till fragrant.
3. Take the pot from temp. then stir in lemon juice, salt, and pepper.
4. Drizzle the lemon garlic sauce over the steamed broccoli prior to serving.

Per serving: Calories: 80 kcal; Fat: 7g; Carbs: 4g; Protein: 2g; Sodium: 10mg; Potassium: 320mg; Phosphorus: 50mg; Calcium: 50mg; Magnesium: 20mg

74. Steamed Edamame with Sea Salt

Preparation time: five mins

Cooking time: five mins

Servings: four

Ingredients:

- two teacups edamame (in pods)
- Sea salt as required

Directions:

1. Boil a pot of water.
2. Include the edamame pods to the boiling water and cook for five mins.
3. Drain the cooked edamame and spray with sea salt.

4. Serve warm or chilled.

Per serving: Calories: 120 kcal; Fat: 5g; Carbs: 9g; Protein: 11g; Sodium: 0mg; Potassium: 610mg; Phosphorus: 190mg; Calcium: 60mg; Magnesium: 60mg

75. Grilled Eggplant with Balsamic Glaze

Preparation time: ten mins

Cooking time: ten mins

Servings: four

Ingredients:

- one big eggplant, sliced into rounds
- two tbsps olive oil
- Salt and pepper as required
- Balsamic glaze for drizzling
- Chopped fresh basil for garnish

Directions:

1. Warm up the grill to moderate-high flame.
2. Brush the eggplant rounds with olive oil then season with salt and pepper.
3. Grill the eggplant rounds for 4-five mins per side till soft and grill marks appear.
4. Bring the grilled eggplant to a serving platter.
5. Drizzle with balsamic glaze then spray with severed fresh basil.
6. Serve warm or at room temp.

Per serving: Calories: 80 kcal; Fat: 6g; Carbs: 7g; Protein: 1g; Sodium: 5mg; Potassium: 230mg; Phosphorus: 30mg; Calcium: 10mg; Magnesium: 15mg

CHAPTER 6
DESSERTS

76. STRAWBERRY BANANA SMOOTHIE   50

77. COCONUT CHIA PUDDING   50

78. QUINOA FRUIT SALAD   50

79. CHIA SEED PUDDING   50

80. RASPBERRY CHIA SEED PUDDING   51

81. BERRY PARFAIT   51

82. PEACH AND RASPBERRY CRISP   51

83. CINNAMON BAKED APPLES   52

84. COCOA BANANA SMOOTHIE BOWL   52

85. FROZEN YOGURT BARK   52

86. WATERMELON FRUIT PIZZA   52

87. GREEK YOGURT WITH HONEY AND NUTS   53

88. BERRY QUINOA PARFAIT   53

89. MANGO COCONUT CHIA POPSICLES   53

90. BAKED APPLE CHIPS   54

76. Strawberry Banana Smoothie

Preparation time: five mins

Cooking time: zero mins

Servings: two

Ingredients:

- one teacup frozen strawberries
- 1 ripe banana
- one teacup unsweetened almond milk
- half teacup nonfat Greek yogurt
- one tbsp honey

Directions:

1. Put frozen strawberries, banana, almond milk, Greek yogurt, and honey inside a mixer.
2. Blend till level and creamy.
3. Pour into glasses and serve instantly.

Per serving: Calories: 120 kcal; Fat: 0g; Carbs: 28gm; Protein: 6g; Sodium: 80mg; Potassium: 420mg; Phosphorus: 110mg; Calcium: 150mg; Magnesium: 25mg

77. Coconut Chia Pudding

Preparation time: five mins

Cooking time: 4 hours (Chilling time)

Servings: two

Ingredients:

- one teacup unsweetened coconut milk
- two tbsps chia seeds
- one tbsp honey or maple syrup
- quarter tsp vanilla extract
- two tbsps unsweetened shredded coconut (optional)

Directions:

1. Inside your container, blend coconut milk, chia seeds, honey or maple syrup, and vanilla extract.
2. Stir thoroughly then let it sit for five mins.
3. Stir again to avoid clumping.
4. Cover the container then put in the fridge for around four hrs or overnight.
5. Serve chilled, topped with unsweetened shredded coconut if anticipated.

Per serving: Calories: 150 kcal; Fat: 11gm; Carbs: 11g; Protein: 3g; Sodium: 10mg; Potassium: 120mg; Phosphorus: 100mg; Calcium: 50mg; Magnesium: 60mg

78. Quinoa Fruit Salad

Preparation time: ten mins

Cooking time: fifteen mins

Servings: four

Ingredients:

- one teacup cooked quinoa
- one teacup mixed fresh fruits (e.g., berries, cubed melon, grapes)
- two tbsps severed mint leaves
- two tbsps lemon juice
- one tbsp honey

Directions:

1. Inside your container, blend cooked quinoa, mixed fruits, severed mint leaves, lemon juice, and honey.
2. Toss gently to mix well.
3. Serve chilled.

Per serving: Calories: 110 kcal; Fat: 0g; Carbs: 25g; Protein: 3g; Sodium: 0mg; Potassium: 130mg; Phosphorus: 60mg; Calcium: 10mg; Magnesium: 30mg

79. Chia Seed Pudding

Preparation time: five mins

Cooking time: 4 hours (Chilling time)

Servings: two

Ingredients:

- two tbsps chia seeds
- one teacup unsweetened almond milk
- one tsp honey or maple syrup
- half tsp vanilla extract
- Fresh berries for topping

Directions:

1. Inside your container, blend chia seeds, almond milk, honey or maple syrup, and vanilla extract.
2. Stir thoroughly then let it sit for five mins.
3. Stir again to avoid clumping.

4. Cover the container then put in the fridge for 4 hours or overnight.

5. Serve chilled, topped with fresh berries.

Per serving: Calories: 100 kcal; Fat: 5g; Carbs: 10g; Protein: 3g; Sodium: 75mg; Potassium: 80mg; Phosphorus: 80mg; Calcium: 180mg; Magnesium: 50mg

80. Raspberry Chia Seed Pudding

Preparation time: five mins

Cooking time: 4 hours (Chilling time)

Servings: two

Ingredients:

- one teacup unsweetened almond milk
- two tbsps chia seeds
- two tbsps honey or maple syrup
- half tsp vanilla extract
- half teacup fresh raspberries

Directions:

1. Inside your container, blend almond milk, chia seeds, honey or maple syrup, and vanilla extract.

2. Stir thoroughly then let it sit for five mins.

3. Stir again to avoid clumping.

4. Cover the container then put in the fridge for around four hrs or overnight.

5. Prior to serving, top with fresh raspberries.

Per serving: Calories: 130 kcal; Fat: 6g; Carbs: 17g; Protein: 3g; Sodium: 0mg; Potassium: 150mg; Phosphorus: 100mg; Calcium: 100mg; Magnesium: 40mg

81. Berry Parfait

Preparation time: ten mins

Cooking time: zero mins

Servings: two

Ingredients:

- one teacup nonfat Greek yogurt
- one teacup mixed berries (strawberries, blueberries, raspberries)
- one tbsp honey
- two tbsps severed nuts (almonds, walnuts)

Directions:

1. In your glass or container, layer yogurt, mixed berries, and honey.

2. Repeat the layers.

3. Top with severed nuts.

4. Serve immediately.

Per serving: Calories: 180 kcal; Fat: 4g; Carbs: 25g; Protein: 14g; Sodium: 60mg; Potassium: 280mg; Phosphorus: 160mg; Calcium: 160mg; Magnesium: 60mg

82. Peach and Raspberry Crisp

Preparation time: ten mins

Cooking time: twenty-five mins

Servings: four

Ingredients:

- two teacups sliced peaches
- one teacup fresh raspberries
- two tbsps honey or maple syrup
- one tbsp lemon juice
- half teacup rolled oats
- quarter teacup almond flour
- two tbsps severed almonds
- two tbsps coconut oil, dissolved
- one tbsp honey or maple syrup
- half tsp cinnamon

Directions:

1. Warm up the oven to 375 deg. F.

2. Inside your container, blend sliced peaches, raspberries, honey or maple syrup, and lemon juice.

3. Toss gently to coat the fruit.

4. In a separate container, mix rolled oats, almond flour, severed almonds, dissolved coconut oil, honey or maple syrup, and cinnamon.

5. Disperse the fruit solution in a baking dish.

6. Distribute the oat solution uniformly across the fruit.

7. Place in the oven then bake for approximately twenty-five mins, or 'til the topping turns a golden-brown color and the fruit starts to bubble.

8. Let cool mildly prior to serving.

Per serving: Calories: 230 kcal; Fat: 10g; Carbs: 34g; Protein: 4g; Sodium: 0mg; Potassium: 230mg; Phosphorus: 70mg; Calcium: 40mg; Magnesium: 40mg

83. Cinnamon Baked Apples

Preparation time: fifteen mins

Cooking time: twenty-five mins

Servings: four

Ingredients:

- 4 medium apples (Granny Smith or Honeycrisp)
- one tbsp honey
- one tsp ground cinnamon
- one tbsp severed walnuts

Directions:

1. Warm up the oven to 375 deg. F.
2. Eliminate the cores from the apples prior to arranging them in a baking dish.
3. Drizzle honey uniformly over the apples.
4. Spray cinnamon and severed walnuts over the top.
5. Bake for twenty-five mins or 'til apples are soft.
6. Serve warm.

Per serving: Calories: 120 kcal; Fat: 1g; Carbs: 28g; Protein: 1g; Sodium: 0mg; Potassium: 190mg; Phosphorus: 20mg; Calcium: 20mg; Magnesium: 8mg

84. Cocoa Banana Smoothie Bowl

Preparation time: five mins

Cooking time: zero mins

Servings: one

Ingredients:

- 1 frozen banana
- half teacup unsweetened almond milk
- two tbsps unsweetened cocoa powder
- one tbsp chia seeds
- one tbsp honey or maple syrup
- Toppings: sliced banana, severed nuts, shredded coconut

Directions:

1. Inside a mixer, blend frozen banana, almond milk, cocoa powder, chia seeds, and honey or maple syrup.
2. Blend till level and creamy.
3. Pour the solution into a container.
4. Top with sliced banana, severed nuts, and shredded coconut.
5. Enjoy with a spoon.

Per serving: Calories: 250 kcal; Fat: 7g; Carbs: 45g; Protein: 5g; Sodium: 60mg; Potassium: 650mg; Phosphorus: 200mg; Calcium: 80mg; Magnesium: 90mg

85. Frozen Yogurt Bark

Preparation time: ten mins

Cooking time: 4 hours (Freezing time)

Servings: four

Ingredients:

- one teacup nonfat Greek yogurt
- two tbsps honey or maple syrup
- half teacup mixed berries (strawberries, blueberries, raspberries)
- two tbsps severed nuts (e.g., almonds, walnuts)

Directions:

1. Inside your container, blend Greek yogurt and honey or maple syrup.
2. Parchment paper should be used to line a baking sheet.
3. Evenly distribute the yogurt solution across the baking tray.
4. Spray mixed berries and severed nuts over the top.
5. Bring the baking tray in the freezer for around four hrs or till firm.
6. Break into pieces and serve.

Per serving: Calories: 80 kcal; Fat: 2g; Carbs: 13g; Protein: 5g; Sodium: 25mg; Potassium: 140mg; Phosphorus: 70mg; Calcium: 70mg; Magnesium: 20mg

86. Watermelon Fruit Pizza

Preparation time: ten mins

Cooking time: zero mins

Servings: 6

Ingredients:

- half watermelon, cut into round slices
- one teacup nonfat Greek yogurt
- one teacup mixed berries (e.g., strawberries, blueberries, raspberries)
- two tbsps honey or maple syrup
- two tbsps severed mint leaves

Directions:

1. Place watermelon slices on a serving platter.
2. Disperse Greek yogurt uniformly over the watermelon slices.
3. Top with mixed berries.
4. Drizzle honey/maple syrup over the fruit.
5. Spray severed mint leaves on top.
6. Slice into wedges and serve.

Per serving: Calories: 70 kcal; Fat: 0g; Carbs: 16g; Protein: 4g; Sodium: 20mg; Potassium: 180mg; Phosphorus: 60mg; Calcium: 50mg; Magnesium: 20mg

87. Greek Yogurt with Honey and Nuts

Preparation time: five mins

Cooking time: zero mins

Servings: one

Ingredients:

- half teacup nonfat Greek yogurt
- one tbsp honey
- one tbsp severed nuts (e.g., almonds, pistachios)

Directions:

1. Inside your container, spoon the Greek yogurt.
2. Drizzle honey over the yogurt.
3. Spray severed nuts on top.
4. Enjoy as a healthy and protein-rich dessert.

Per serving: Calories: 150 kcal; Fat: 4g; Carbs: 20g; Protein: 12g; Sodium: 75mg; Potassium: 210mg; Phosphorus: 150mg; Calcium: 120mg; Magnesium: 50mg

88. Berry Quinoa Parfait

Preparation time: ten mins

Cooking time: fifteen mins

Servings: two

Ingredients:

- half teacup cooked quinoa
- one teacup mixed berries (e.g., strawberries, blueberries, raspberries)
- half teacup nonfat Greek yogurt
- two tbsps honey or maple syrup
- two tbsps severed nuts (e.g., almonds, walnuts)

Directions:

1. Inside a glass or jar, layer cooked quinoa, mixed berries, Greek yogurt, honey or maple syrup, and severed nuts.
2. Repeat the layers 'til all the components are used.
3. Serve immediately or put in the fridge 'til ready to eat.

Per serving: Calories: 200 kcal; Fat: 5g; Carbs: 32g; Protein: 9g; Sodium: 35mg; Potassium: 260mg; Phosphorus: 140mg; Calcium: 110mg; Magnesium: 50mg

89. Mango Coconut Chia Popsicles

Preparation time: ten mins

Cooking time: 4 hours (Freezing time)

Servings: 6

Ingredients:

- one teacup cubed mango
- one teacup unsweetened coconut milk
- two tbsps chia seeds
- two tbsps honey or maple syrup

Directions:

1. Inside a mixer, blend cubed mango, coconut milk, chia seeds, and honey or maple syrup.
2. Blend till level and well combined.
3. Pour the solution into popsicle molds.
4. Introduce popsicle sticks then freeze for around four hrs or till solid.
5. Eliminate from the molds and relish.

Per serving: Calories: 90 kcal; Fat: 4g; Carbs: 15g; Protein: 2g; Sodium: 0mg; Potassium:

140mg; Phosphorus: 50mg; Calcium: 40mg; Magnesium: 20mg

90. Baked Apple Chips

Preparation time: ten mins

Cooking time: two hrs

Servings: four

Ingredients:

- 2 apples
- one tsp ground cinnamon

Directions:

1. Warm up the oven to 200 deg. F.
2. Slice the apples finely, around one-eighth inch thick.
3. Arrange the apple slices onto a baking tray that has been covered with parchment paper.
4. Spray cinnamon uniformly over the apple slices.
5. Turn the slices over after an hour in the oven. Bake for another hour.
6. Take from the oven then let cool completely.
7. Store in a sealed container.

Per serving: Calories: 60 kcal; Fat: 0gm; Carbs: 16gm; Protein: 0gm; Sodium: 0mg; Potassium: 100mg; Phosphorus: 10mg; Calcium: 10mg; Magnesium: 5mg

CHAPTER 7
DRINKS

91. Berry Blast Smoothie 56

92. Matcha Green Tea Latte 56

93. Mango Basil Smoothie 56

94. Kiwi Spinach Smoothie 56

95. Sparkling Lemonade 57

96. Orange Carrot Ginger Juice 57

97. Pineapple Coconut Smoothie 57

98. Blueberry Spinach Smoothie 57

99. Pomegranate Mint Cooler 57

100. Beetroot Carrot Juice 58

101. Raspberry Lime Spritzer 58

102. Green Detox Juice 58

103. Mango Turmeric Smoothie 59

104. Pineapple Ginger Turmeric Smoothie 59

105. Blueberry Almond Smoothie 59

91. Berry Blast Smoothie

Preparation time: five mins

Cooking time: zero mins

Servings: one

Ingredients:

- half teacup unsweetened almond milk
- half teacup mixed berries (such as strawberries, blueberries, and raspberries)
- half teacup low-fat yogurt
- one tsp honey or stevia (optional)
- Ice cubes

Directions:

1. Inside a mixer, blend the mixed berries, almond milk, yogurt, and sweetener if anticipated.
2. Blend till level and creamy.
3. Pour into a glass over ice cubes.

Per serving: Calories: 100 kcal; Fat: 2g; Carbs: 16g; Protein: 5g; Sodium: 110mg; Potassium: 210mg; Phosphorus: 130mg; Calcium: 200mg; Magnesium: 20mg

92. Matcha Green Tea Latte

Preparation time: five mins

Cooking time: five mins

Servings: one

Ingredients:

- one tsp matcha green tea powder
- quarter teacup hot water
- three-quarter teacup unsweetened almond milk
- one tsp honey or stevia (optional)

Directions:

1. Inside your container, whisk the matcha powder with hot water till dissolved and frothy.
2. In your small saucepan, temp. the almond milk across moderate flame 'til hot but not boiling.
3. Pour the hot almond milk into a cup, then include the matcha solution.
4. Stir in honey or stevia if anticipated.
5. Enjoy the matcha latte warm.

Per serving: Calories: 50 kcal; Fat: 2g; Carbs: 6g; Protein: 2g; Sodium: 150mg; Potassium: 150mg; Phosphorus: 60mg; Calcium: 200mg; Magnesium: 30mg

93. Mango Basil Smoothie

Preparation time: five mins

Cooking time: zero mins

Servings: one

Ingredients:

- one teacup mango chunks
- half teacup low-fat plain yogurt
- quarter teacup fresh basil leaves
- one tsp honey or stevia (optional)
- Ice cubes

Directions:

1. Inside a mixer, blend the mango chunks, yogurt, basil leaves, and honey or stevia (if utilizing).
2. Blend till level and creamy.
3. Pour into a glass over ice cubes.

Per serving: Calories: 150 kcal; Fat: 1g; Carbs: 34g; Protein: 5g; Sodium: 70mg; Potassium: 460mg; Phosphorus: 140mg; Calcium: 180mg; Magnesium: 40mg

94. Kiwi Spinach Smoothie

Preparation time: five mins

Cooking time: zero mins

Servings: one

Ingredients:

- 2 kiwis, skinned and sliced
- one teacup fresh spinach
- half teacup unsweetened coconut water
- half teacup low-fat Greek yogurt
- Ice cubes

Directions:

1. Inside a mixer, blend the kiwis, spinach, coconut water, and Greek yogurt.
2. Blend till level and creamy.
3. Pour into a glass over ice cubes.

Per serving: Calories: 130 kcal; Fat: 1g; Carbs: 28g; Protein: 6g; Sodium: 90mg;

Potassium: 680mg; Phosphorus: 140mg; Calcium: 100mg; Magnesium: 65mg

95. Sparkling Lemonade

Preparation time: five mins

Cooking time: zero mins

Servings: one

Ingredients:

- one teacup sparkling water
- Juice of 1 lemon
- one tsp honey or stevia (optional)
- Ice cubes

Directions:

1. Inside a glass, blend the sparkling water and lemon juice.
2. Include honey or stevia if anticipated and stir well.
3. Serve over ice cubes.

Per serving: Calories: 15 kcal; Fat: 0gm; Carbs: 4g; Protein: 0gm; Sodium: 0mg; Potassium: 22mg; Phosphorus: 1mg; Calcium: 6mg; Magnesium: 3mg

96. Orange Carrot Ginger Juice

Preparation time: ten mins

Cooking time: zero mins

Servings: two

Ingredients:

- 4 oranges, skinned
- two big carrots, skinned
- one-inch piece of ginger, skinned

Directions:

1. In a juicer or blender, process the oranges, carrots, and ginger till well combined.
2. Strain the juice if anticipated.
3. Pour into glasses and serve chilled.

Per serving: Calories: 100 kcal; Fat: 0g; Carbs: 24g; Protein: 2g; Sodium: 10mg; Potassium: 460mg; Phosphorus: 50mg; Calcium: 80mg; Magnesium: 25mg

97. Pineapple Coconut Smoothie

Preparation time: five mins

Cooking time: zero mins

Servings: one

Ingredients:

- one teacup pineapple chunks
- half teacup unsweetened coconut milk
- half teacup low-fat Greek yogurt
- one tsp honey or stevia (optional)
- Ice cubes

Directions:

1. Inside your mixer, blend the pineapple chunks, coconut milk, Greek yogurt, and honey or stevia (if utilizing).
2. Blend till level and creamy.
3. Pour into a glass over ice cubes.

Per serving: Calories: 120 kcal; Fat: 3g; Carbs: 18g; Protein: 8g; Sodium: 50mg; Potassium: 380mg; Phosphorus: 190mg; Calcium: 90mg; Magnesium: 45mg

98. Blueberry Spinach Smoothie

Preparation time: five mins

Cooking time: zero mins

Servings: one

Ingredients:

- half teacup blueberries
- one teacup fresh spinach
- half banana
- half teacup almond milk
- one tbsp chia seeds
- Ice cubes

Directions:

1. Inside a mixer, blend the blueberries, spinach, banana, almond milk, and chia seeds.
2. Blend till level.
3. Pour into a glass over ice cubes.

Per serving: Calories: 150 kcal; Fat: 4g; Carbs: 28g; Protein: 4g; Sodium: 95mg; Potassium: 400mg; Phosphorus: 120mg; Calcium: 240mg; Magnesium: 70mg

99. Pomegranate Mint Cooler

Preparation time: ten mins

Cooking time: zero mins

Servings: two

Ingredients:

- one teacup pomegranate seeds
- Juice of 1 lemon
- one tbsp honey or stevia (optional)
- 10-12 fresh mint leaves
- two teacups sparkling water
- Ice cubes

Directions:

1. Inside a mixer, blend the pomegranate seeds, lemon juice, honey or stevia (if utilizing), and mint leaves.
2. Blend till level.
3. In glasses, split the blended solution equally.
4. Include ice cubes then top with sparkling water.
5. Stir gently and serve chilled.

Per serving: Calories: 60 kcal; Fat: 0g; Carbs: 15g; Protein: 1g; Sodium: 10mg; Potassium: 190mg; Phosphorus: 10mg; Calcium: 20mg; Magnesium: 15mg

100. Beetroot Carrot Juice

Preparation time: ten mins

Cooking time: zero mins

Servings: two

Ingredients:

- one average beetroot, skinned and severed
- two average carrots, skinned and severed
- one apple, cored and severed
- one-inch piece of ginger, skinned
- half lemon, skinned
- Ice cubes

Directions:

1. In a juicer or blender, process the beetroot, carrots, apple, ginger, and lemon till well combined.
2. Strain the juice if anticipated.
3. Pour into glasses and serve chilled.

Per serving: Calories: 80 kcal; Fat: 0g; Carbs: 20g; Protein: 2g; Sodium: 60mg; Potassium: 520mg; Phosphorus: 40mg; Calcium: 30mg; Magnesium: 30mg

101. Raspberry Lime Spritzer

Preparation time: five mins

Cooking time: zero mins

Servings: one

Ingredients:

- half teacup raspberries
- Juice of 1 lime
- one teacup sparkling water
- one tsp honey or stevia (optional)
- Ice cubes

Directions:

1. In a glass, muddle the raspberries with the back of a spoon to release their juices.
2. Include the lime juice, sparkling water, and honey or stevia (if utilizing).
3. Stir thoroughly to blend.
4. Serve over ice cubes.

Per serving: Calories: 20 kcal; Fat: 0g; Carbs: 5g; Protein: 0g; Sodium: 0mg; Potassium: 75mg; Phosphorus: 1mg; Calcium: 20mg; Magnesium: 5mg

102. Green Detox Juice

Preparation time: ten mins

Cooking time: zero mins

Servings: one

Ingredients:

- one teacup spinach
- half cucumber, skinned
- one green apple, cored
- half lemon, skinned
- one-inch piece of ginger, skinned
- one teacup water

Directions:

1. In a juicer or blender, blend the entire components.
2. Process till level and well blended.
3. Pour into a glass and serve.

Per serving: Calories: 80 kcal; Fat: 0g; Carbs: 20g; Protein: 2g; Sodium: 15mg; Potassium:

580mg; Phosphorus: 45mg; Calcium: 50mg; Magnesium: 40mg

103. Mango Turmeric Smoothie

Preparation time: five mins

Cooking time: zero mins

Servings: one

Ingredients:

- one teacup mango chunks
- half tsp ground turmeric
- half teacup unsweetened almond milk
- half teacup low-fat Greek yogurt
- one tbsp honey or stevia (optional)
- Ice cubes

Directions:

1. Inside a mixer, blend the mango chunks, ground turmeric, almond milk, Greek yogurt, and honey or stevia (if utilizing).
2. Blend till level and creamy.
3. Pour into a glass over ice cubes.

Per serving: Calories: 150 kcal; Fat: 2g; Carbs: 30g; Protein: 6g; Sodium: 85mg; Potassium: 460mg; Phosphorus: 135mg; Calcium: 110mg; Magnesium: 45mg

104. Pineapple Ginger Turmeric Smoothie

Preparation time: ten mins

Cooking time: zero mins

Servings: one

Ingredients:

- one teacup pineapple chunks
- half tsp grated ginger
- half tsp ground turmeric
- half teacup coconut water
- half teacup low-fat Greek yogurt
- Ice cubes

Directions:

1. Inside a mixer, blend the pineapple chunks, grated ginger, ground turmeric, coconut water, and Greek yogurt.
2. Blend till level and creamy.
3. Pour into a glass over ice cubes.

Per serving: Calories: 140 kcal; Fat: 1g; Carbs: 30g; Protein: 6g; Sodium: 85mg; Potassium: 540mg; Phosphorus: 125mg; Calcium: 90mg; Magnesium: 45mg

105. Blueberry Almond Smoothie

Preparation time: five mins

Cooking time: zero mins

Servings: one

Ingredients:

- one teacup blueberries
- one teacup unsweetened almond milk
- quarter teacup low-fat Greek yogurt
- one tbsp almond butter
- one tsp honey or stevia (optional)
- Ice cubes

Directions:

1. Inside a mixer, blend the blueberries, almond milk, Greek yogurt, almond butter, and honey or stevia (if utilizing).
2. Blend till level and creamy.
3. Pour into a glass over ice cubes.

Per serving: Calories: 180 kcal; Fat: 6g; Carbs: 25g; Protein: 9g; Sodium: 170mg; Potassium: 340mg; Phosphorus: 220mg; Calcium: 260mg; Magnesium: 80mg

CHAPTER 8
QUICK AND EASY MEALS

106. Spinach and Mushroom Omelette   61

107. Chicken Chili   61

108. Turkey and Vegetable Skewers   61

109. Mediterranean Pork   62

110. Baked Cod with Herbed Crust   62

111. Caramelized Pork Chops   63

112. Turkey Meatballs with Marinara Sauce   63

113. Baked Salmon with Asparagus   63

114. Mediterranean Pasta Salad   64

115. Baked Chicken Breast with Roasted Vegetables   64

116. Veggie Quesadillas   64

117. Eggplant Parmesan   65

118. Quinoa Stuffed Bell Peppers   65

119. Lentil Soup   66

120. Greek Yogurt Parfait   66

106. Spinach and Mushroom Omelette

Preparation time: five mins

Cooking time: ten mins

Servings: one

Ingredients:

- 2 eggs
- quarter teacup severed spinach
- quarter teacup sliced mushrooms
- two tbsps cubed onion
- quarter teacup shredded mozzarella cheese
- Salt and pepper as required
- one tsp olive oil

Directions:

1. Inside your container, beat the eggs. Season with salt and pepper.
2. Warm the olive oil in your non-stick griddle across moderate flame.
3. Include the spinach, mushrooms, & onion to the griddle. Sauté till the vegetables are softened.
4. Pour the beaten eggs into the griddle, swirling to distribute them uniformly.
5. Spray the shredded mozzarella cheese over one half of the omelette.
6. Cook for a few minutes 'til the eggs are set and the cheese is dissolved.
7. Wrap the omelette in half and transfer it to a plate.
8. Serve warm.

Per serving: Calories: 300 kcal; Fat: 20gm; Carbs: 10g; Protein: 20g; Sodium: 400mg; Potassium: 500mg; Phosphorus: 250mg; Calcium: 200mg; Magnesium: 40mg

107. Chicken Chili

Preparation time: fifteen mins

Cooking time: twenty mins

Servings: 10

Ingredients:

- four tbsps extra-virgin olive oil
- six pieces garlic, crushed
- two average green bell peppers, severed
- two big onions, severed
- four teacups cubed sweet potatoes
- 4 teaspoons ground cumin
- 4 tablespoons chili powder
- 2 teaspoon dried oregano
- 2 cans (15oz/425g each) of low-sodium cannellini beans, washed
- two teacups frozen corn
- 1 ½ teaspoons salt
- four teacups chicken stock
- four teacups cooked, cubed chicken
- ½ teaspoon pepper or as required

To serve:

- Sour cream
- Chopped cilantro
- Avocado, skinned, pitted, severed

Directions:

1. Whisk oil into a big soup pot and temp. across the flame. When the oil is heated, include garlic & onion then cook for some mins.
2. Stir in sweet potatoes and bell pepper and cook till vegetables are mildly cooked. Include spices and oregano and stir for a couple of secs 'til you get a nice aroma.
3. Stir in beans and broth. Slow down the temp., cover the pot partially and cook for around twenty mins when it begins to boil. Include corn and cook for some mins. Stir in chicken and temp. thoroughly.
4. Turn off the temp.. Include salt and pepper and stir. Ladle into containers.
5. Serve with suggested toppings.

Per serving: Calories: 365kcal; Carbs: 47g; Protein: 15g; Fat: 13g; Sodium: 551mg; Potassium: 480mg; Phosphorus: 65mg; Calcium: 45mg; Magnesium: 33mg

108. Turkey and Vegetable Skewers

Preparation time: fifteen mins

Cooking time: fifteen mins

Servings: four

Ingredients:

- one lb. turkey breast, cut into cubes
- one bell pepper, cut into chunks
- one zucchini, cut into rounds
- one red onion, cut into chunks
- two tbsps olive oil
- one tbsp lemon juice
- one tsp dried oregano
- Salt and pepper as required

Directions:

1. Warm the grill or grill pot beforehand to medium-high temp..
2. Inside your container, blend olive oil, lemon juice, dried oregano, salt, and pepper.
3. Skewer pieces of red onion, bell pepper, zucchini, and cubes of turkey.
4. Apply the olive oil solution onto the skewers using a brush.
5. Cook the skewers on the grill, turning them occasionally, for ten to twelve mins or till the turkey is thoroughly cooked.
6. Serve warm.

Per serving: Calories: 200 kcal; Fat: 6g; Carbs: 10g; Protein: 25g; Sodium: 200mg; Potassium: 500mg; Phosphorus: 250mg; Calcium: 30mg; Magnesium: 40mg

109. Mediterranean Pork

Preparation time: ten mins

Cooking time: thirty-five mins

Servings: two

Ingredients:

- two pork chops (bone-in)
- half tsp salt pepper as required
- one and half garlic pieces (skinned and crushed)
- half tsp dried rosemary

Directions:

1. Warm up the oven to 425 deg. F. Sprinkle on the pork chops with salt and pepper. Include rosemary and garlic to them in a roasting pot.

2. Cook for ten mins in the oven and afterwards diminish the temp. to 350 F then roast for another twenty-five mins.
3. Pork chops should be sliced and served on plates. Drizzle the pot liquid all over the place. Serve.

Per serving: Calories: 335kcal; Carbs: 1.52g; Protein: 40.48g; Fat: 17.42g; Sodium: 126mg; Potassium: 330mg; Phosphorus: 230mg; Calcium: 13mg; Magnesium: 23mg

110. Baked Cod with Herbed Crust

Preparation time: ten mins

Cooking time: fifteen mins

Servings: two

Ingredients:

- 2 cod fillets
- quarter teacup breadcrumbs
- one tbsp severed fresh parsley
- one tbsp severed fresh dill
- one tbsp grated Parmesan cheese
- one tbsp olive oil
- one tbsp lemon juice
- Salt and pepper as required

Directions:

1. Warm up the oven to 400 deg. F.
2. Bring the cod fillets on a baking tray lined with parchment paper.
3. In your small container, blend breadcrumbs, severed parsley, severed dill, grated Parmesan cheese, olive oil, lemon juice, salt, and pepper. Mix thoroughly.
4. Disperse the breadcrumb solution evenly over the cod fillets, pressing mildly to adhere.
5. Bake for twelve-fifteen mins or 'til the fish is cooked through then flakes simply with a fork.
6. Serve warm.

Per serving: Calories: 200 kcal; Fat: 6g; Carbs: 10g; Protein: 25g; Sodium: 300mg; Potassium: 500mg; Phosphorus: 200mg; Calcium: 100mg; Magnesium: 50mg

111. Caramelized Pork Chops

Preparation time: five mins

Cooking time: thirty mins

Servings: two

Ingredients:

- 2 pounds of pork chops
- one tsp salt
- one tsp pepper
- two tbsps chili powder
- ½ teaspoon olive oil
- two oz. green chili (severed)
- quarter tsp dried oregano
- quarter tsp ground cumin
- one garlic clove (crushed)
- one onion (sliced)
- ½ glass of water

Directions:

1. Sprinkle half tsp pepper, half tsp seasoned salt, chili powder, oregano, and cumin over the pork chops. Then, temp. half tsp of oil and the garlic across moderate flame in a pot.
2. Cook the pork chops on both sides. Toss in the onion and water in the griddle. Cover afterwards diminish the temp. to low, then cook for approximately twenty mins.
3. Turn the loins over then season with the remaining pepper and salt. Cover then cook till the liquid has evaporated & the onions are medium brown.
4. Eliminate the chops from the pot. Serve with a sprinkling of onions on top.

Per serving: Calories: 500kcal; Carbs: 4g; Protein: 27g; Fat: 19g; Sodium: 86mg; Potassium: 160mg; Phosphorus: 116mg; Calcium: 38mg; Magnesium: 14mg

112. Turkey Meatballs with Marinara Sauce

Preparation time: fifteen mins

Cooking time: twenty mins

Servings: four

Ingredients:

- one lb. ground turkey
- quarter teacup breadcrumbs
- quarter teacup grated Parmesan cheese
- quarter teacup severed fresh parsley
- 1 egg, beaten
- two pieces garlic, crushed
- one tsp dried oregano
- half tsp salt
- quarter tsp black pepper
- two teacups low-sodium marinara sauce

Directions:

1. Warm up the oven to 375 deg. F.
2. Inside a huge container, blend ground turkey, breadcrumbs, Parmesan cheese, parsley, egg, garlic, oregano, salt, and pepper. Mix thoroughly.
3. Form the solution into meatballs that are approximately 1 inch in size.
4. Arrange the meatballs on a baking tray that has been lined with parchment paper.
5. Cook in the oven for twenty mins or 'til they are fully cooked.
6. In a distinct saucepot, temp. the marinara sauce.
7. Serve the turkey meatballs with the marinara sauce.

Per serving: Calories: 250 kcal; Fat: 10g; Carbs: 15gm; Protein: 25g; Sodium: 600mg; Potassium: 500mg; Phosphorus: 200mg; Calcium: 150mg; Magnesium: 40mg

113. Baked Salmon with Asparagus

Preparation time: ten mins

Cooking time: fifteen mins

Servings: two

Ingredients:

- two salmon fillets
- one bunch of asparagus
- two tsps olive oil
- Salt and pepper as required

Directions:

1. Warm up the oven to 400 deg. F.
2. Bring the salmon fillets on a baking tray then spray with olive oil. Season with salt and pepper.

3. Trim the asparagus and place it on the baking tray with the salmon.

4. Bake for fifteen mins or 'til the salmon is cooked through then the asparagus is soft.

5. Serve warm.

Per serving: Calories: 300 kcal; Fat: 15gm; Carbs: 5gm; Protein: 30g; Sodium: 100mg; Potassium: 700mg; Phosphorus: 300mg; Calcium: 50mg; Magnesium: 50mg

114. Mediterranean Pasta Salad

Preparation time: fifteen mins

Cooking time: ten mins

Servings: four

Ingredients:

- eight oz. pasta
- one teacup cherry tomatoes, shared
- one teacup cubed cucumber
- half teacup cubed red onion
- half teacup Kalamata olives, pitted & shared
- quarter teacup crumbled feta cheese
- two tbsps severed fresh basil
- two tbsps lemon juice
- two tbsps olive oil
- Salt and pepper as required

Directions:

1. Cook the pasta as per to package directions. Drain and wash with cold water.

2. Inside a huge container, combine the cooked pasta, cherry tomatoes, cucumber, red onion, Kalamata olives, feta cheese, basil, olive oil, lemon juice, salt, and pepper. Toss thoroughly to combine.

3. Serve chilled.

Per serving: Calories: 300 kcal; Fat: 10g; Carbs: 45g; Protein: 10g; Sodium: 400mg; Potassium: 300mg; Phosphorus: 150mg; Calcium: 100mg; Magnesium: 30mg

115. Baked Chicken Breast with Roasted Vegetables

Preparation time: ten mins

Cooking time: thirty mins

Servings: two

Ingredients:

- 2 boneless, skinless chicken breasts
- two teacups assorted vegetables (broccoli, carrots, cauliflower)
- two tbsps olive oil
- one tsp dried thyme
- one tsp garlic powder
- Salt and pepper as required

Directions:

1. Warm up the oven to 400 deg. F.

2. Bring the chicken breasts on a baking tray lined with parchment paper. Drizzle with olive oil then spray with dried thyme, garlic powder, salt, and pepper.

3. In a separate container, toss the mixed vegetables with olive oil, salt, and pepper.

4. Place the vegetables on the baking tray alongside the chicken breasts.

5. Bake for 25-thirty mins or 'til the chicken is cooked through & the vegetables are soft.

6. Serve warm.

Per serving: Calories: 300 kcal; Fat: 10g; Carbs: 15g; Protein: 30g; Sodium: 400mg; Potassium: 800mg; Phosphorus: 250mg; Calcium: 80mg; Magnesium: 50mg

116. Veggie Quesadillas

Preparation time: ten mins

Cooking time: ten mins

Servings: two

Ingredients:

- 4 tortillas
- one teacup shredded cheddar cheese
- half teacup cubed bell peppers
- half teacup cubed zucchini
- half teacup cubed tomatoes
- quarter teacup cubed red onion
- two tbsps severed cilantro
- Salt and pepper as required
- Salsa and Greek yogurt for serving

Directions:

1. Place two tortillas on a flat surface. Sprinkle half of the shredded cheddar cheese evenly on each tortilla.

2. Inside your container, combine bell peppers, zucchini, tomatoes, red onion, cilantro, salt, and pepper. Mix thoroughly.

3. Distribute the vegetable solution evenly onto both tortillas, spreading it over the cheese.

4. Arrange the remaining two tortillas on the vegetable solution, gently pressing them down.

5. Warm a big griddle across moderate flame. Cook each quesadilla for approximately 3-four mins on every end 'til the cheese is dissolved and the tortillas turn a golden brown.

6. Slice the quesadillas into triangular pieces and accompany them with salsa and Greek yogurt.

Per serving: Calories: 350 kcal; Fat: 15g; Carbs: 35g; Protein: 20g; Sodium: 500mg; Potassium: 400mg; Phosphorus: 200mg; Calcium: 400mg; Magnesium: 40mg

117. Eggplant Parmesan

Preparation time: fifteen mins

Cooking time: forty mins

Servings: four

Ingredients:

- one big eggplant, sliced into rounds
- one teacup breadcrumbs
- quarter teacup grated Parmesan cheese
- two eggs, whisked
- two teacups low-sodium marinara sauce
- one teacup shredded mozzarella cheese
- two tbsps severed fresh basil
- Salt and pepper as required
- Olive oil for frying

Directions:

1. Warm up the oven to 375 deg. F.

2. Begin by submerging the eggplant slices in the beaten eggs, then proceed to coat them with a combination of breadcrumbs, grated Parmesan cheese, salt, and pepper.

3. Take a big griddle and temp. up some olive oil across moderate flame. Proceed to fry the breaded eggplant slices till they turn a golden-brown hue on both sides. Afterwards, drain them on paper towels.

4. Within your baking dish, apply a thin layer of marinara sauce. Next, arrange a layer of the fried eggplant slices on top.

5. Continue the layering process by alternating between marinara sauce, eggplant slices, and shredded mozzarella cheese till all the components have been used.

6. Put the baking dish in the oven and bake for approximately thirty mins, or 'til the cheese has fully dissolved and is visibly bubbling.

7. Garnish with severed fresh basil prior to serving.

Per serving: Calories: 300 kcal; Fat: 15g; Carbs: 25g; Protein: 15g; Sodium: 600mg; Potassium: 500mg; Phosphorus: 300mg; Calcium: 350mg; Magnesium: 50mg

118. Quinoa Stuffed Bell Peppers

Preparation time: fifteen mins

Cooking time: thirty mins

Servings: four

Ingredients:

- 4 bell peppers, tops removed and seeds removed
- one teacup cooked quinoa
- one teacup black beans, washed and drained
- one teacup corn kernels
- one teacup cubed tomatoes
- half teacup shredded cheddar cheese
- one tsp chili powder
- half tsp cumin
- Salt and pepper as required

Directions:

1. Warm up the oven to 375 deg. F.

2. Inside a huge container, combine cooked quinoa, black beans, corn kernels, cubed tomatoes, shredded cheddar cheese, chili powder, cumin, salt, and pepper.

3. Spoon the quinoa solution into the bell peppers and place them in a baking dish.

4. Bake for 25-thirty mins 'til the peppers are soft and the filling is heated over.

5. Serve warm.

Per serving: Calories: 300 kcal; Fat: 8g; Carbs: 45g; Protein: 15g; Sodium: 400mg; Potassium: 600mg; Phosphorus: 250mg; Calcium: 200mg; Magnesium: 70mg

119. Lentil Soup

Preparation time: ten mins

Cooking time: thirty mins

Servings: four

Ingredients:

- one teacup dried lentils
- four teacups low-sodium vegetable broth
- one onion, severed
- 2 carrots, cubed
- 2 stalks celery, cubed
- two pieces garlic, crushed
- one tsp cumin
- half tsp paprika
- quarter tsp turmeric
- Salt and pepper as required
- two tbsps severed fresh parsley
- one tbsp lemon juice

Directions:

1. Wash the lentils below cold water.

2. Inside a big pot, blend lentils, vegetable broth, onion, carrots, celery, garlic, cumin, paprika, turmeric, salt, and pepper.

3. Boil solution across high temp. Diminish temp. to low, cover, simmer for twenty-five to thirty mins or 'til the lentils are soft.

4. Stir in severed parsley and lemon juice.

5. Serve warm.

Per serving: Calories: 250 kcal; Fat: 1g; Carbs: 45g; Protein: 15g; Sodium: 400mg; Potassium: 800mg; Phosphorus: 250mg; Calcium: 80mg; Magnesium: 50mg

120. Greek Yogurt Parfait

Preparation time: five mins

Cooking time: zero mins

Servings: one

Ingredients:

- half teacup plain Greek yogurt
- quarter teacup fresh berries (strawberries, blueberries, raspberries)
- two tbsps granola
- one tbsp honey

Directions:

1. In your glass or container, layer plain Greek yogurt, fresh berries, and granola.

2. Drizzle honey on top.

3. Serve chilled.

Per serving: Calories: 200 kcal; Fat: 4gm; Carbs: 30g; Protein: 15g; Sodium: 80mg; Potassium: 300mg; Phosphorus: 200mg; Calcium: 150mg; Magnesium: 20mg

CHAPTER 9
VEGETARIAN/VEGAN OPTIONS

121. Quinoa and Vegetable Stir-Fry   68

122. Summer Vegetable Sauté   68

123. Sweet Potato and Black Bean Chili   68

124. Mediterranean Quinoa Bowl   69

125. Chickpea and Vegetable Stew   69

126. Ratatouille   69

127. Veggie Lentil Burgers   70

128. Chickpea and Vegetable Curry   70

129. Veggie and Brown Rice Stir-Fry   71

130. Healthy Vegetable Fried Rice   71

131. Vegetable and Lentil Curry   72

132. Cauliflower and Potato Curry   72

133. Greek Salad   73

134. Mediterranean Chickpea Salad   73

135. Lentil and Vegetable Stir-Fried Rice   73

121. Quinoa and Vegetable Stir-Fry

Preparation time: ten mins

Cooking time: twenty mins

Servings: four

Ingredients:

- one teacup quinoa, cooked
- one tbsp olive oil
- one onion, sliced
- two pieces garlic, crushed
- one bell pepper, sliced
- one zucchini, sliced
- one teacup broccoli florets
- one teacup snap peas
- two tbsps low-sodium soy sauce
- one tbsp sesame oil
- one tbsp rice vinegar
- 1 tsp. agave syrup or sweetener of choice

Directions:

1. Warm olive oil inside a big griddle or wok across moderate flame.
2. Include onion and garlic, sauté till fragrant and translucent.
3. Include bell pepper, zucchini, broccoli, and snap peas. Stir-fry for five to seven mins, or till vegetables are soft-crisp.
4. Include cooked quinoa to the griddle.
5. In your small container, whisk simultaneously soy sauce, sesame oil, rice vinegar, and agave syrup. Pour the sauce over the quinoa & vegetables. Stir well to coat.
6. Cook for an additional two to three mins, 'til everything is temp.ed through.
7. Serve warm.

Per serving: Calories: 290 kcal; Fat: 12g; Carbs: 40g; Protein: 8g; Sodium: 470mg; Potassium: 520mg; Phosphorus: 160mg; Calcium: 40mg; Magnesium: 80mg

122. Summer Vegetable Sauté

Preparation time: ten mins

Cooking time: fifteen mins

Servings: 6

Ingredients:

- two tbsps margarine
- two teacups sliced zucchini
- one-eighth tsp garlic powder
- half teacup cubed green pepper
- one ten-oz package of frozen corn (thawed)
- two tbsps severed pimiento
- one-eighth tsp pepper

Directions:

1. Inside a big griddle, melt margarine.
2. Include the other components then cook for approximately fifteen mins or 'til the vegetables are soft.

Per serving: Calories: 81kcal; Carbs: 9gm; Protein: 2gm; Fat: 4gm; Sodium: 312mg; Potassium: 357mg; Phosphorus: 143mg; Calcium: 30mg; Magnesium: 27mg

123. Sweet Potato and Black Bean Chili

Preparation time: fifteen mins

Cooking time: thirty mins

Servings: four

Ingredients:

- one tbsp olive oil
- one onion, severed
- two pieces garlic, crushed
- two sweet potatoes, skinned and cubed
- one bell pepper, cubed
- one tin black beans, washed and drained
- one tin cubed tomatoes
- two teacups vegetable broth
- two tsps chili powder
- one tsp cumin
- Salt and pepper as required
- Fresh cilantro for garnish

Directions:

1. Warm olive oil inside a big pot across moderate flame.
2. Include onion and garlic, sauté till fragrant and translucent.
3. Include sweet potatoes and bell pepper, cook for five mins, blending occasionally.

4. Include black beans, cubed tomatoes, vegetable broth, chili powder, cumin, salt, and pepper. Raise to a boil.

5. Lower the temp. then simmer for twenty mins, till sweet potatoes are soft.

6. Serve warm, garnished with fresh cilantro.

Per serving: Calories: 280 kcal; Fat: 4g; Carbs: 55g; Protein: 10g; Sodium: 550mg; Potassium: 900mg; Phosphorus: 200mg; Calcium: 90mg; Magnesium: 80mg

124. Mediterranean Quinoa Bowl

Preparation time: fifteen mins

Cooking time: twenty mins

Servings: four

Ingredients:

- one teacup quinoa, cooked
- one teacup cherry tomatoes, shared
- one cucumber, cubed
- half red onion, thinly sliced
- quarter teacup Kalamata olives, pitted & shared
- quarter teacup crumbled feta cheese (substitute with vegan feta if anticipated)
- two tbsps fresh lemon juice
- two tbsps olive oil
- two tbsps severed fresh dill
- Salt and pepper as required

Directions:

1. Inside a huge container, combine cooked quinoa, cherry tomatoes, cucumber, red onion, Kalamata olives, and feta cheese.

2. In your small container, whisk simultaneously lemon juice, olive oil, dill, salt, and pepper.

3. Drizzle the dressing across the quinoa solution then toss to combine.

4. Serve chilled or at room temp.

Per serving: Calories: 280 kcal; Fat: 12g; Carbs: 35g; Protein: 9g; Sodium: 350mg; Potassium: 500mg; Phosphorus: 200mg; Calcium: 100mg; Magnesium: 90mg

125. Chickpea and Vegetable Stew

Preparation time: ten mins

Cooking time: thirty mins

Servings: four

Ingredients:

- two tbsps olive oil
- one onion, severed
- two pieces garlic, crushed
- 1 carrot, cubed
- 1 celery stalk, cubed
- one bell pepper, cubed
- one zucchini, cubed
- one can chickpeas, washed and drained
- 1 can cubed tomatoes
- two teacups vegetable broth
- one tsp dried thyme
- Salt and pepper as required
- Fresh parsley for garnish

Directions:

1. Warm olive oil inside a big pot across moderate flame.

2. Include onion and garlic, sauté till fragrant and translucent.

3. Include carrot, celery, bell pepper, and zucchini. Cook for five mins, blending occasionally.

4. Include chickpeas, cubed tomatoes, vegetable broth, dried thyme, salt, and pepper. Raise to a boil.

5. Lower the temp. then simmer for twenty mins, till vegetables are soft.

6. Serve warm, garnished with fresh parsley.

Per serving: Calories: 230 kcal; Fat: 7g; Carbs: 35g; Protein: 9g; Sodium: 500mg; Potassium: 600mg; Phosphorus: 180mg; Calcium: 90mg; Magnesium: 60mg

126. Ratatouille

Preparation time: fifteen mins

Cooking time: forty mins

Servings: four

Ingredients:

- two tbsps olive oil
- one onion, sliced
- three pieces garlic, crushed
- one eggplant, cubed
- one zucchini, cubed
- one yellow squash, cubed
- one red bell pepper, cubed
- one can cubed tomatoes
- one tsp dried thyme
- one tsp dried oregano
- Salt and pepper as required
- Fresh basil for garnish

Directions:

1. Warm olive oil inside a big griddle across moderate flame.
2. Include onion and garlic, sauté till fragrant and translucent.
3. Include eggplant, zucchini, yellow squash, and bell pepper. Cook for ten mins, stirring occasionally.
4. Include cubed tomatoes, dried thyme, dried oregano, salt, and pepper. Stir well.
5. Diminish temp. to low, cover, simmer for thirty mins, till vegetables are soft.
6. Serve warm, garnished with fresh basil.

Per serving: Calories: 180 kcal; Fat: 8gm; Carbs: 25g; Protein: 4g; Sodium: 280mg; Potassium: 600mg; Phosphorus: 90mg; Calcium: 40mg; Magnesium: 50mg

127. Veggie Lentil Burgers

Preparation time: fifteen mins

Cooking time: twenty mins

Servings: four

Ingredients:

- one teacup cooked lentils
- half teacup breadcrumbs (use gluten-free breadcrumbs if anticipated)
- quarter teacup finely severed onion
- quarter teacup grated carrot
- quarter teacup severed bell pepper
- quarter teacup severed fresh parsley

- two pieces garlic, crushed
- two tbsps tomato paste
- one tbsp soy sauce
- one tsp ground cumin
- Salt and pepper as required
- 4 whole wheat burger buns (or gluten-free buns)
- Toppings of choice (lettuce, tomato, onion, etc.)

Directions:

1. Inside a huge container, mash the cooked lentils with a fork or potato masher.
2. Include breadcrumbs, onion, carrot, bell pepper, parsley, garlic, tomato paste, soy sauce, cumin, salt, and pepper. Mix thoroughly to combine.
3. Form the solution into 4 burger patties.
4. Warm up some olive oil in your griddle on moderate flame.
5. Allow the burger patties to cook for approximately 4-five mins on every end 'til they are nicely browned and heated all the way through.
6. Serve the lentil burgers on whole wheat buns with your choice of toppings.

Per serving: Calories: 220 kcal; Fat: 2g; Carbs: 39g; Protein: 12g; Sodium: 480mg; Potassium: 560mg; Phosphorus: 200mg; Calcium: 50mg; Magnesium: 60mg

128. Chickpea and Vegetable Curry

Preparation time: fifteen mins

Cooking time: thirty mins

Servings: four

Ingredients:

- one tbsp olive oil
- one onion, severed
- two pieces garlic, crushed
- one bell pepper, cubed
- one zucchini, cubed
- one teacup cubed eggplant
- one can chickpeas, washed and drained
- 1 can coconut milk

- two tbsps curry powder
- one tsp turmeric
- Salt and pepper as required
- Fresh cilantro for garnish

Directions:

1. Warm olive oil inside a big pot across moderate flame.
2. Include onion and garlic, sauté till fragrant and translucent.
3. Include bell pepper, zucchini, and eggplant. Cook for five mins, stirring occasionally.
4. Include chickpeas, coconut milk, curry powder, turmeric, salt, and pepper. Raise to a boil.
5. Lower the heat then simmer for twenty to twenty-five mins, 'til the vegetables are soft and the curry has densed.
6. Serve warm, garnished with fresh cilantro.

Per serving: Calories: 340 kcal; Fat: 16g; Carbs: 40g; Protein: 10g; Sodium: 390mg; Potassium: 750mg; Phosphorus: 220mg; Calcium: 80mg; Magnesium: 80mg

129. Veggie and Brown Rice Stir-Fry

Preparation time: fifteen mins

Cooking time: twenty mins

Servings: four

Ingredients:

- two teacups cooked brown rice
- two tbsps low-sodium soy sauce
- one tbsp sesame oil
- one tbsp rice vinegar
- one tsp agave syrup or sweetener of choice
- one tbsp olive oil
- one onion, sliced
- two pieces garlic, crushed
- one bell pepper, sliced
- one zucchini, sliced
- one teacup broccoli florets
- one teacup snap peas

Directions:

1. In your small container, whisk simultaneously soy sauce, sesame oil, rice vinegar, and agave syrup. Put away.
2. Warm olive oil inside a big griddle or wok across moderate flame.
3. Include onion and garlic, sauté till fragrant and translucent.
4. Include bell pepper, zucchini, broccoli, and snap peas. Stir-fry for five to seven mins, or till vegetables are soft-crisp.
5. Include cooked brown rice to the griddle and pour the sauce over the vegetables and rice. Stir well to coat.
6. Cook for an additional two to three mins, 'til everything is heated through.
7. Serve warm.

Per serving: Calories: 280 kcal; Fat: 10gm; Carbs: 40g; Protein: 7g; Sodium: 450mg; Potassium: 600mg; Phosphorus: 170mg; Calcium: 60mg; Magnesium: 60mg

130. Healthy Vegetable Fried Rice

Preparation time: fifteen mins

Cooking time: ten mins

Servings: four

Ingredients:

For the Sauce:

- one-third teacup of garlic vinegar
- 1 and 1/two tbsps of molasses
- one tsp of onion powder

For the Fried Rice:

- one tsp of olive oil
- 2 mildly beaten whole eggs + 4 egg whites
- one teacup of mixed vegetable
- one teacup of edamame
- two teacups of brown rice (cooked)

Directions:

1. Make the sauce by blending the garlic vinegar, molasses, and onion powder in a glass jar. Shake well. Warm-up oil in a big wok or griddle across moderate-high flame.
2. Include eggs and egg whites, and let cook till the eggs set for about 1 minute. Break up eggs with a spatula or spoon

into small pieces. Include frozen mixed vegetables and frozen edamame.

3. Cook for four mins, blending regularly. Include the brown rice and sauce to the vegetable-and-egg solution. Cook for five mins or 'til heated through. Serve immediately.

Per serving: Calories: 390kcal; Carbs: 56g; Protein: 8g; Fat: 17g; Sodium: 42mg; Potassium: 601mg; Phosphorus: 494mg; Calcium: 89mg; Magnesium: 101mg

131. Vegetable and Lentil Curry

Preparation time: twenty mins

Cooking time: forty mins

Servings: four

Ingredients:

- one tbsp olive oil
- one onion, severed
- two pieces garlic, crushed
- 1 bell pepper, cubed
- one zucchini, cubed
- one teacup cubed eggplant
- one teacup severed cauliflower
- one teacup cooked lentils
- 1 can coconut milk
- two tbsps curry powder
- one tsp turmeric
- Salt and pepper as required
- Fresh cilantro for garnish

Directions:

1. Warm olive oil inside a big pot across moderate flame.

2. Include onion and garlic, sauté till fragrant and translucent.

3. Include bell pepper, zucchini, eggplant, and cauliflower. Cook for five mins, stirring occasionally.

4. Include cooked lentils, coconut milk, curry powder, turmeric, salt, and pepper. Raise to a boil.

5. Diminish the temp. then simmer for thirty mins, 'til the vegetables are soft and the curry has thickened.

6. Serve hot, garnished with fresh cilantro.

Per serving: Calories: 280 kcal; Fat: 12g; Carbs: 32g; Protein: 11g; Sodium: 380mg; Potassium: 780mg; Phosphorus: 240mg; Calcium: 70mg; Magnesium: 90mg

132. Cauliflower and Potato Curry

Preparation time: ten mins

Cooking time: fifteen mins

Servings: four

Ingredients:

- two tbsps of oil
- ½ onion, severed
- 2-inch piece of ginger
- 3 garlic cloves
- one tsp of turmeric
- one tsp of cumin
- one small cauliflower
- one average potato
- 2 small tomatoes
- one small green chili
- ½ cup of water
- Juice of lemon
- ¼ cup of cilantro (leaves)
- one tsp of garam masala
- Rice or bread (for serving)

Directions:

1. Warm and cook in a saucepan or fry pot on moderate flame. Cook, constantly stirring, till the onion is softened. Fry it till ginger and garlic are fragrant.

2. Pour the turmeric and cumin and mix well. Toss the cauliflower, potato, tomatoes, chili, and water in a container and whisk. Carry to a gentle simmer, then lower to low heat and cover.

3. Cook for twenty-five mins, stirring periodically, till the potatoes and cauliflower are cooked. Combine the lemon juice, cilantro, and garam masala inside a blending container.

4. Serve with rice or toast as a side dish.

Per serving: Calories: 387kcal; Carbs: 42g; Protein: 17g; Fat: 15.7g; Sodium: 557mg; Potassium: 682mg; Phosphorus: 311mg; Calcium: 93mg; Magnesium: 88mg

133. Greek Salad

Preparation time: fifteen mins

Cooking time: zero mins

Servings: four

Ingredients:

- four teacups mixed salad greens
- one cucumber, cubed
- one teacup cherry tomatoes, shared
- 1/2 red onion, thinly sliced
- quarter teacup Kalamata olives, pitted & shared
- quarter teacup crumbled feta cheese (substitute with vegan feta if anticipated)
- two tbsps extra virgin olive oil
- two tbsps red wine vinegar
- one tsp dried oregano
- Salt and pepper as required

Directions:

1. Inside a big salad container, combine mixed salad greens, cucumber, cherry tomatoes, red onion, Kalamata olives, and feta cheese.
2. Combine olive oil, dried oregano, red wine vinegar, salt, & pepper in a small container, whisking them simultaneously.
3. Drizzle the dressing across the salad then toss to combine.
4. Present the dish promptly.

Per serving: Calories: 180 kcal; Fat: 14g; Carbs: 10g; Protein: 4g; Sodium: 310mg; Potassium: 300mg; Phosphorus: 80mg; Calcium: 120mg; Magnesium: 30mg

134. Mediterranean Chickpea Salad

Preparation time: fifteen mins

Cooking time: zero mins

Servings: four

Ingredients:

- two tins chickpeas, washed and drained
- one cucumber, cubed
- one teacup cherry tomatoes, shared
- 1/2 red onion, thinly sliced
- quarter teacup Kalamata olives, pitted & shared
- quarter teacup crumbled feta cheese (substitute with vegan feta if anticipated)
- two tbsps fresh lemon juice
- two tbsps olive oil
- two tbsps severed fresh parsley
- Salt and pepper as required

Directions:

1. Inside a huge container, combine chickpeas, cucumber, Kalamata olives, cherry tomatoes, red onion, and feta cheese.
2. In your small container, whisk simultaneously lemon juice, olive oil, parsley, salt, and pepper.
3. Drizzle the dressing across the chickpea solution and toss to combine.
4. Serve chilled or at room temp.

Per serving: Calories: 320 kcal; Fat: 12g; Carbs: 42g; Protein: 12g; Sodium: 580mg; Potassium: 650mg; Phosphorus: 210mg; Calcium: 120mg; Magnesium: 80mg

135. Lentil and Vegetable Stir-Fried Rice

Preparation time: fifteen mins

Cooking time: twenty mins

Servings: four

Ingredients:

- two teacups cooked brown rice, chilled
- one tbsp olive oil
- one onion, severed
- two pieces garlic, crushed
- 1 bell pepper, cubed
- 1 carrot, cubed
- one teacup frozen peas
- one teacup cooked lentils
- two tbsps low-sodium soy sauce
- one tbsp sesame oil
- one tsp grated fresh ginger
- Salt and pepper as required
- Optional toppings: severed green onions, toasted sesame seeds

Directions:

1. Warm olive oil inside a big griddle or wok across moderate flame.

2. Include onion and garlic, sauté till fragrant and translucent.

3. Include bell pepper, carrot, and frozen peas. Stir-fry for five mins, or 'til vegetables are soft-crisp.

4. Include cooked lentils and chilled brown rice. Stir-fry for another five mins, breaking up any clumps of rice.

5. In your small container, whisk simultaneously soy sauce, sesame oil, grated ginger, salt, and pepper. Pour the sauce over the rice mixture. Stir well to coat.

6. Cook for an additional two to three mins, 'til everything is heated through.

7. Serve hot, topped with severed green onions then toasted sesame seeds if anticipated.

Per serving: Calories: 320 kcal; Fat: 10gm; Carbs: 47g; Protein: 13gm; Sodium: 450mg; Potassium: 550mg; Phosphorus: 230mg; Calcium: 60mg; Magnesium: 60mg

CHAPTER 10
SPECIAL OCCASIONS

136. GRILLED VEGETABLE PASTA — 76

137. BROCCOLI AND BEAN CASSEROLE — 76

138. MEDITERRANEAN CHICKEN SKEWERS — 76

139. GRILLED PINEAPPLE WITH YOGURT AND HONEY — 77

140. TACO-SEASONED ROAST BEEF WRAPS — 77

141. SESAME SALMON WITH BROCCOLI AND TOMATOES — 77

142. MUSSELS WITH CREAMY TARRAGON SAUCE — 78

143. GINGER AND CHILI BAKED FISH — 78

144. SPINACH FALAFEL WRAP — 79

145. PRESSURE COOKER LENTIL SLOPPY JOES WITH COLESLAW — 79

146. SWEDISH SPICY CARROT WITH COD — 80

147. GRILLED SALMON WITH PAPAYA-MINT SALSA — 81

148. LEMON HERB ROASTED TURKEY BREAST — 81

149. BAKED POTATO — 81

150. GRILLED VEGETABLE SKEWERS WITH TOFU — 82

136. Grilled Vegetable Pasta

Preparation time: fifteen mins

Cooking time: fifteen mins

Servings: four

Ingredients:

- eight oz. whole wheat pasta
- one zucchini, sliced
- one yellow squash, sliced
- one red bell pepper, sliced
- one red onion, sliced
- two tbsps olive oil
- two pieces garlic, crushed
- one tsp dried basil
- one tsp dried oregano
- Salt and pepper as required
- Grated Parmesan cheese for serving

Directions:

1. Cook the pasta as per to the package instructions. Drain and put away.
2. Warm up the grill to moderate-high flame.
3. In a huge container, toss the sliced zucchini, red bell pepper, yellow squash, and red onion with olive oil, crushed garlic, dried basil, dried oregano, salt, and pepper.
4. Grill the vegetables for about 5-7 minutes, mixing irregularly, 'til they are soft and mildly charred.
5. Inside a huge serving container, combine the grilled vegetables and cooked pasta. Toss to combine.
6. Serve the grilled vegetable pasta with a spray of grated Parmesan cheese, if anticipated.

Per serving: Calories: 300 kcal; Fat: 10gm; Carbs: 45g; Protein: 10g; Sodium: 100mg; Potassium: 500mg; Phosphorus: 150mg; Calcium: 40mg; Magnesium: 40mg

137. Broccoli and Bean Casserole

Preparation time: ten mins

Cooking time: thirty-five mins

Servings: four

Ingredients:

- ¾ cup vegetable broth or water
- 2 broccoli heads
- one tsp salt
- two cups cooked pinto or navy beans, or one (fourteen oz.) can
- one to two tbsps brown rice flour or arrowroot flour
- one teacup walnuts

Directions:

1. Warm up the oven to 350 deg. F. Warm the broth in a big ovenproof saucepan across moderate flame.
2. Include the broccoli and season with salt. 6–eight mins, or till the broccoli is brilliant green. Combine the pinto beans and brown rice flour in a mixing container.
3. Cook for another five mins, or 'til the liquid has mildly thickened. Over the top, scatter the walnuts. Warm up the oven to 350 deg. F then bake the pot for 20 to twenty-five mins.
4. Toasted walnuts are recommended.

Per serving: Calories: 410kcal; Carbs: 43g; Protein: 22g; Fat: 20g; Sodium: 635mg; Potassium: 866mg; Phosphorus: 605mg; Calcium: 40mg; Magnesium: 35mg

138. Mediterranean Chicken Skewers

Preparation time: twenty mins

Cooking time: fifteen mins

Servings: four

Ingredients:

- one zucchini, sliced
- one yellow squash, sliced
- one red bell pepper, cut into chunks
- one lb. boneless, skinless chicken breasts, cut into chunks
- one red onion, cut into wedges
- quarter teacup olive oil
- two tbsps lemon juice
- two pieces garlic, crushed
- one tbsp dried oregano
- Salt and pepper as required

Directions:

1. Warm up the grill to moderate-high flame.

2. Inside your container, whisk simultaneously the olive oil, lemon juice, crushed garlic, dried oregano, salt, and pepper.

3. Thread the chicken chunks, zucchini, yellow squash, red bell pepper, and red onion onto skewers, alternating between the components.

4. Brush the skewers with the prepared marinade, making sure to coat all sides.

5. Grill the chicken skewers for about 8-ten mins, mixing irregularly, 'til the chicken is cooked through and no longer pink in the middle.

6. Serve the Mediterranean chicken skewers with a side of couscous or a Greek salad.

Per serving: Calories: 250 kcal; Fat: 10g; Carbs: 10g; Protein: 30g; Sodium: 150mg; Potassium: 600mg; Phosphorus: 250mg; Calcium: 40mg; Magnesium: 40mg

139. Grilled Pineapple with Yogurt and Honey

Preparation time: ten mins

Cooking time: six mins

Servings: four

Ingredients:

- one huge pineapple, skinned, cored, and cut into thick rings
- one teacup plain Greek yogurt
- two tbsps honey
- one tsp vanilla extract
- Fresh mint leaves for garnish

Directions:

1. Warm up the grill/grill pot to moderate flame.

2. Put the pineapple rings on the grill then cook for around 3 mins on every end, 'til they have grill marks and are mildly caramelized.

3. In your small container, whisk simultaneously the Greek yogurt, honey, and vanilla extract 'til well combined.

4. Eliminate the grilled pineapple rings from the grill and let them cool mildly.

5. Serve the grilled pineapple rings with a dollop of the yogurt and honey mixture on top.

6. Garnish with fresh mint leaves.

7. Enjoy the grilled pineapple as a light and refreshing dessert option.

Per serving: Calories: 150 kcal; Fat: 1gm; Carbs: 35g; Protein: 5gm; Sodium: 50mg; Potassium: 400mg; Phosphorus: 100mg; Calcium: 80mg; Magnesium: 30mg

140. Taco-Seasoned Roast Beef Wraps

Preparation time: ten mins

Cooking time: zero mins

Servings: two

Ingredients:

- two tbsps low-fat cream cheese
- two (ten-inch) flour tortillas
- 4 ounces low-sodium roast beef
- ½ cup fresh spinach
- one tsp Taco Seasoning
- two tbsps cubed red onion
- two tbsps pimento or cherry pepper (shared lengthwise)

Directions:

1. Put one tbsp of cream cheese on one tortilla and top with taco seasoning.

2. Top with 1four teacups spinach, one tbsp red onion, one tbsp pimento pepper and two oz. roast meat.

Per serving: Calories: 278kcal; Carbs: 27g; Protein: 18g; Fat: 11g; Sodium: 116mg; Potassium: 261mg; Phosphorus: 296mg; Calcium: 74mg; Magnesium: 30mg

141. Sesame Salmon with Broccoli and Tomatoes

Preparation time: thirty mins

Cooking time: twenty-five mins

Servings: two

Ingredients:

- two tsps rapeseed oil
- 2 pieces of salmon fillets
- 6 spring onions
- 12 tomatoes
- 1 2/3 cups broccoli, trimmed
- one tbsp soya sauce
- one tsp Sesame oil
- ½ teaspoon crushed dried chili flakes
- one tsp sesame seeds

Directions:

1. Warm up the oven to 400 deg F. Drizzle the oil over a baking tray. Put the salmon fillets down in the tray, along with the spring onions and tomatoes, and season generously with ground black pepper.

2. Heated the oven to 350 deg F and bake for eight mins. In the meantime, fill a pot halfway with water and raise it to a boil. Return the pot to a boil with the broccoli.

3. Drain after 4 minutes of cooking. Place the broccoli on the baking tray after removing it from the oven.

4. Soya sauce and sesame oil should be drizzled over the fish. Revert the salmon to the oven for the next 3 to 4 minutes, or till just done, then spray with the chili powder and sesame seeds.

5. Split it up between two heated plates to serve.

Per serving: Calories: 224kcal; Carbs: 20g; Protein: 17g; Fat: 21g; Sodium: 196mg; Potassium: 875mg; Phosphorus: 440mg; Calcium: 42mg; Magnesium: 22mg

142. Mussels with Creamy Tarragon Sauce

Preparation time: twenty mins

Cooking time: twenty-five mins

Servings: two

Ingredients:

- 2 pounds fresh, live mussels
- one tbsp olive oil
- one average leek, trimmed and finely cut(around 100 grams prepared weight)
- two garlic pieces, skinned and finely cut

- ½ cup dry white wine
- 5 tablespoons full-Protein: crème fraiche
- three-four fresh tarragon stalks (around 1 tsp), leaves picked and roughly severed
- one tsp dried tarragon

Directions:

1. Eliminate the 'beards' by dumping the mussels into the sink and scrubbing them thoroughly under cold running water. Mussels with fractured shells or those that do not close when pounded on the sink's side should be discarded. Drain the ones that are good in a colander.

2. Warm the oil over low heat in a deep, lidded, wide-based saucepan or shallow casserole. Gently sauté the leek and garlic for two to three mins, or till softened but not browned.

3. Season generously with salt and pepper after adding the white wine, crème Fraiche, and tarragon. Bring the wine to a simmer by increasing the heat under the pot. Cook for around four mins, or 'til most of the mussels have steamed open, after stirring in the mussels and covering closely with a lid.

4. Stir thoroughly, then cover and cook for another one to two mins, or 'til the rest of the vegetables are done.

5. Eliminate any mussels that haven't opened, split the mussels between two containers, and pour the tarragon broth over the top.

Per serving: Calories: 381kcal; Carbs: 4g; Protein: 27g; Fat: 2g; Sodium: 236mg; Potassium: 971mg; Phosphorus: 598mg; Calcium: 83mg; Magnesium: 24mg

143. Ginger and Chili Baked Fish

Preparation time: thirty mins

Cooking time: forty mins

Servings: one

Ingredients:

- 2 teaspoon olive oil
- 6 ounces thick white fish fillet,
- 1 garlic clove, peeled and thinly sliced
- 3 teaspoons of stem ginger

- 1 spring onion
- 1 red bird's eye chili,
- ½ small lime
- Handful fresh coriander leaves

Directions:

1. Warm up the oven to 400 deg F. Drizzle the oil over a rectangle of kitchen foil on a baking tray. Place the fish on half of the foil, skin side down, with enough foil to cover it. Garlic, ginger, spring onion, and chili are sprinkled over the fish, and lime juice is squeezed over it.

2. Toss the fish with salt and black pepper prior to folding the foil over it and rolling up the edges to seal it within. Because steam is required to cook the fish, make sure the package isn't too tight. Oven warmed up to 350 deg F and bake the fish for approximately twenty mins, or till a fork pierces the fish and it flakes into big pieces.

3. Using a fish slice or spatula, carefully open the foil bundle and lift the fish onto a warming platter. Serve the fish with the cooking fluids, lots of fresh coriander, and lime wedges on the side.

Per serving: Calories: 233kcal; Carbs: 7g; Protein: 31g; Fat: 11g; Sodium: 346mg; Potassium: 441mg; Phosphorus: 342mg; Calcium: 41mg; Magnesium: 42mg

144. Spinach Falafel Wrap

Preparation time: ten mins

Cooking time: fifteen mins

Servings: four

Ingredients:

- 6 ounces spinach
- 1 Can chickpeas
- two tsps of ground cumin
- ¾ cup of flour
- two tbsps of canola oil for frying
- ¼ cup of plain yogurt
- two garlic pieces
- Juice of 1 lemon
- Black pepper
- 4 tortillas
- 1 cucumber
- 2 slices onion

- Salad greens (for serving)

Directions:

1. To whither the spinach, please place it in a colander in the sink then pour boiling water over it. Allow cooling prior to pressing as much water as possible out of the spinach. Toss the spinach, chickpeas, cumin, and flour in a food processor.

2. Pulse till everything is well combined. Spoon the mixture into tablespoon-size balls and flatten them into patties with your palms. One tablespoon oil, heated in a large pot over moderate-high flame. Sauté for some minutes on every end, or till browned and crisp, using half of the falafel patties.

3. Carry on with the remaining falafel patties in the same manner. Combine the yogurt, garlic, lemon juice, and pepper in a small container. Place 3 falafel patties, a few cucumber spears, a few red onion rings, and a handful of salad leaves on each tortilla. one tbsp yogurt sauce on top of each.

Per serving: Calories: 700.78kcal; Carbs: 34.91g; Protein: 4.12g; Fat: 4.79g; Sodium: 136mg; Potassium: 806mg; Phosphorus: 248mg; Calcium: 221mg; Magnesium: 123mg

145. Pressure Cooker Lentil Sloppy Joes with Coleslaw

Preparation time: five mins

Cooking time: thirty-five mins

Servings: 8

Ingredients:

- one average onion (cubed)
- one average red bell pepper (cubed)
- two garlic pieces (crushed)
- one tsp avocado oil
- two teacups low-sodium or no-salt-added vegetable broth
- one (15-oz.) can of low-sodium or no-salt-included cubed tomatoes
- two tbsps low-sodium or no-salt-included tomato paste
- one tbsp maple syrup
- one tsp coconut amino

- one tbsp Low-Sodium Dijon Mustard or store-bought
- one tsp (smoked) paprika
- one tsp chili powder
- one teacup dry lentils (green or brown), rinsed
- one tsp ground cumin
- one tsp freshly squeezed lemon juice
- 6 whole-wheat hamburger buns

For Coleslaw

- two tbsps Low-Sodium Dijon Mustard or store-bought
- two tbsps apple cider vinegar
- four teacups bagged coleslaw mix
- quarter tsp black pepper

Directions:

1. Select the sauté setting on high in the pressure cooker. For 3 minutes, sauté the oil, onion, bell pepper, and garlic till the veggies are soft.

2. Combine the broth, tomatoes and juices, lentils, tomato paste, maple syrup, mustard, paprika, chili powder, cumin, lemon juice, and coconut amino in a large mixing container. Stir continuously and combine well.

3. Close the cover and cook for fifteen mins under high pressure.

For Coleslaw

4. Meanwhile, whisk the mustard, vinegar, and black pepper in a medium mixing container. Toss in the coleslaw mildly. Allow fifteen mins for the pressure to relax naturally. Release any residual pressure manually.

5. Distribute the lentil mixture between the buns. Coleslaw may be served on the side or on top of the sloppy joes.

6. Put in the fridge the remaining lentil mixture for up to 1 week or freeze it for 3 months in an airtight container.

Per serving: Calories: 320kcal; Carbs: 51g; Protein: 15.5g; Fat: 5g; Sodium: 286mg; Potassium: 586mg; Phosphorus: 348mg; Calcium: 41mg; Magnesium: 39mg

146. Swedish Spicy Carrot with Cod

Preparation time: 30minutes

Cooking time: thirty-five mins

Servings: two

Ingredients:

- two big carrots (around 11 ounces), trimmed and thickly sliced
- 1 garlic clove, peeled
- 3 teaspoons fresh root ginger, peeled
- 3 teaspoons butter
- ½ tablespoon fresh lemon juice
- 5 ounces thick, skinless cod fillets (or other white fish)
- one tbsp olive oil
- Good pinch dried chili flakes

Directions:

1. Take a medium saucepan and include the carrots, garlic, and ginger to the water. Raise to a boil, then lower the heat and cook for fifteen mins, or 'til the vegetables are soft. Eliminate the carrot, garlic, and ginger from the pot, scoop out, set aside a ladleful of water (half teacup), and drain.

2. Return the potatoes to the pot with 3 tablespoons of the cooking liquid, the butter, and the lemon juice. Using a stick blender, blitz the carrots till they're a level, creamy purée, applying a little more boiling water if required. To taste, stir with salt and black pepper.

3. Take it out of the equation. Coat the fish fillets on both sides with salt & black pepper. Warm the oil in a greased frying pot across moderate flame. After adding the fish, cook for 4 minutes. Turn the fish over, spray with a few chili flakes, and cook for 3–five mins more, depending on the thickness of each fillet. When the cod begins to flake into huge chunks, it is ready.

4. Place the purée on two warmed plates and top with the fish.

Per serving: Calories: 244kcal; Carbs: 33g; Protein: 12g; Fat: 19g; Sodium: 116mg; Potassium: 898mg; Phosphorus: 413mg; Calcium: 72mg; Magnesium: 45mg

147. Grilled Salmon with Papaya-Mint Salsa

Preparation time: ten mins

Cooking time: forty mins

Servings: four

Ingredients:

- 4 salmon steaks
- quarter teacup papaya
- quarter teacup bell pepper
- one tsp fresh ginger
- one tbsp pimiento
- one tbsp fresh mint
- one tbsp rice wine or white vinegar
- one tbsp fresh lime juice
- ¼ cup green onion
- one tsp jalapeño pepper
- Vegetable oil cooking spray

Directions:

1. Inside a container, include and mix the entire components for the salsa, except the salmon. Put in the fridge round about thirty mins after covering.

2. Cooking Oil the grill or broiler pot mildly.

3. Sauté the salmon on both sides with pepper. five mins on every end on the grill or under the broiler, or till done. quarter teacup salsa on top of each salmon steak.

Per serving: Calories: 194kcal; Carbs: 3g; Protein: 25g; Fat: 8.9g; Sodium: 116mg; Potassium: 733mg; Phosphorus: 699mg; Calcium: 41mg; Magnesium: 52mg

148. Lemon Herb Roasted Turkey Breast

Preparation time: fifteen mins

Cooking time: one hr thirty mins

Servings: 6

Ingredients:

- one (four to five lbs.) bone-in turkey breast
- 2 lemons, juiced and zested
- two tbsps olive oil
- two pieces garlic, crushed
- one tbsp dried thyme
- one tbsp dried rosemary
- Salt and pepper as required

Directions:

1. Warm up the oven to 325 deg. F then line a roasting pot with foil.

2. In your small container, combine the lemon juice, lemon zest, olive oil, crushed garlic, dried thyme, dried rosemary, salt, and pepper. Mix well.

3. Place the turkey breast in the prepared roasting pot and brush it with the lemon herb mixture, making sure to coat all sides.

4. Roast the turkey breast in the warmed up oven for approximately one hr & thirty mins, or 'til the internal temp. reaches 165 deg. F.

5. Eliminate the turkey breast from the oven then let it rest for 10-15 mins prior to slicing.

6. Serve the lemon herb roasted turkey breast with a side of roasted vegetables or quinoa.

Per serving: Calories: 300 kcal; Fat: 10g; Carbs: 2g; Protein: 45g; Sodium: 200mg; Potassium: 500mg; Phosphorus: 400mg; Calcium: 80mg; Magnesium: 60mg

149. Baked Potato

Preparation time: ten mins

Cooking time: fifteen mins

Servings: four

Ingredients:

- 1 medium potato
- one-third teacup of flour
- one tin of black beans
- half teacup onion
- 3/4 teaspoon apple cider
- half tsp of chili powder
- one teacup greens
- one teacup panko for coating
- quarter teacup olive oil
- 4 buns
- one tsp of garlic powder
- Pinch of salt

Toppings:

- Avocado, mustard, greens, and tomato

Directions:

1. Cook the potato and combine it with the black beans in a mash.

2. Continue to mash with a fork after adding the onion, vinegar, garlic powder, chili powder, salt, flour, and greens.

3. Coat patties with panko and form them into four patties. Fry in a frying pot or saucepan and serve with your favorite toppings.

Per serving: Calories: 365kcal; Carbs: 62g; Protein: 15g; Fat: 2g; Sodium: 146mg; Potassium: 781mg; Phosphorus: 358mg; Calcium: 42mg; Magnesium: 50mg

150. Grilled Vegetable Skewers with Tofu

Preparation time: twenty mins

Cooking time: fifteen mins

Servings: four

Ingredients:

- one block firm tofu, cut into cubes
- one zucchini, sliced
- one yellow squash, sliced
- one red bell pepper, cut into chunks
- one green bell pepper, cut into chunks
- one red onion, cut into wedges
- two tbsps olive oil
- two tbsps balsamic vinegar
- one tsp dried oregano
- Salt and pepper as required

Directions:

1. Warm up the grill to moderate-high flame.

2. Inside your container, whisk simultaneously the olive oil, balsamic vinegar, dried oregano, salt, and pepper.

3. Thread the tofu cubes and vegetables onto skewers, alternating between tofu and vegetables.

4. Brush the skewers with the prepared marinade, making sure to coat all sides.

5. Grill the vegetable skewers for about 8-ten mins, mixing irregularly, 'til the vegetables are tender and mildly charred.

6. Serve the grilled vegetable skewers with a side of brown rice or quinoa.

Per serving: Calories: 180 kcal; Fat: 10g; Carbs: 12g; Protein: 12g; Sodium: 150mg; Potassium: 500mg; Phosphorus: 200mg; Calcium: 150mg; Magnesium: 60mg

12 - Weeks Meal Plan

Week 1

Days	Breakfast	Lunch	Dinner	Dessert	Nutrition
1	Whole Wheat Banana Pancakes	Turkey and Avocado Wrap	Turkey Meatballs with Whole Wheat Pasta	Cinnamon Baked Apples	Sodium: 1160mg Potassium: 1440mg
2	Green Smoothie Bowl	Caprese Salad	Pork with Dates Sauce	Frozen Yogurt Bark	Sodium: 781mg Potassium: 1799mg
3	Overnight Chia Pudding	Greek Quinoa Salad	Lentil and Vegetable Curry	Quinoa Fruit Salad	Sodium: 790mg Potassium: 1330mg
4	Sweet Potato Hash with Eggs	Chicken Chop Suey	Salmon with Quinoa and Steamed Broccoli	Coconut Chia Pudding	Sodium: 670mg Potassium: 2090mg
5	Quinoa Breakfast Bowl	Caprese Pasta Salad	Spiced Up Pork Chops	Greek Yogurt with Honey and Nuts	Sodium: 481mg Potassium: 1352mg
6	Spinach and Feta Omelette	Lentil and Vegetable Soup	Pork and Sweet Potatoes	Cocoa Banana Smoothie Bowl	Sodium: 1169mg Potassium: 2300mg
7	Smashed Avocado Toast	Greek Turkey Burgers	Grilled Veggie and Halloumi Skewers	Peach and Raspberry Crisp	Sodium: 1120mg Potassium: 1480mg

Week 2

Days	Breakfast	Lunch	Dinner	Dessert	Nutrition
1	Cottage Cheese and Fruit Bowl	Pork and Pumpkin Chili	Grilled Chicken with Roasted Sweet Potatoes and Green Beans	Berry Parfait	Sodium: 909mg Potassium: 2035mg
2	Whole Grain Breakfast Burrito	Mediterranean Tuna Salad	Vegetable Lentil Soup	Mango Coconut Chia Popsicles	Sodium: 1420mg Potassium: 1560mg
3	Yogurt and Berry Smoothie	Oven Fried Chicken	Herbed Butter Pork Chops	Baked Apple Chips	Sodium: 488mg Potassium: 951mg
4	Spinach and Feta Breakfast Wrap	Pork Chops and Apples	Turkey and Vegetable Stir-Fry	Berry Quinoa Parfait	Sodium: 1111mg Potassium: 1735mg
5	Smoked Salmon Breakfast Toast	Tuna Salad Lettuce Wraps	Baked Salmon with Quinoa and Roasted Vegetables	Strawberry Banana Smoothie	Sodium: 1010mg Potassium: 1390mg
6	Avocado and Egg Toast	Ground Beef and Bell Peppers	Baked Cod with Lemon-Herb Quinoa	Watermelon Fruit Pizza	Sodium: 796mg Potassium: 2008mg
7	Berry Chia Pudding	Greek Chickpea Salad	Baked Cod with Quinoa and Steamed Asparagus	Chia Seed Pudding	Sodium: 855mg Potassium: 1380mg

Week 3

Days	Breakfast	Lunch	Dinner	Dessert	Nutrition
1	Chia Seed Pudding with Berries	Cajun Pork Chops	Chicken Stir-Fry with Brown Rice	Raspberry Chia Seed Pudding	Sodium: 786mgm Potassium: 1372mg
2	Whole Wheat Banana Pancakes	Turkey and Avocado Wrap	Turkey Meatballs with Whole Wheat Pasta	Cinnamon Baked Apples	Sodium: 1160mg Potassium: 1440mg
3	Green Smoothie Bowl	Caprese Salad	Pork with Dates Sauce	Frozen Yogurt Bark	Sodium: 781mg Potassium: 1799mg
4	Overnight Chia Pudding	Greek Quinoa Salad	Lentil and Vegetable Curry	Quinoa Fruit Salad	Sodium: 790mg Potassium: 1330mg
5	Sweet Potato Hash with Eggs	Chicken Chop Suey	Salmon with Quinoa and Steamed Broccoli	Coconut Chia Pudding	Sodium: 670mg Potassium: 2090mg
6	Quinoa Breakfast Bowl	Caprese Pasta Salad	Spiced Up Pork Chops	Greek Yogurt with Honey and Nuts	Sodium: 481mg Potassium: 1352mg
7	Spinach and Feta Omelette	Lentil and Vegetable Soup	Pork and Sweet Potatoes	Cocoa Banana Smoothie Bowl	Sodium: 1169mg Potassium: 2300mg

Week 4

Days	Breakfast	Lunch	Dinner	Dessert	Nutrition
1	Smashed Avocado Toast	Greek Turkey Burgers	Grilled Veggie and Halloumi Skewers	Peach and Raspberry Crisp	Sodium: 1120mg Potassium: 1480mg
2	Cottage Cheese and Fruit Bowl	Pork and Pumpkin Chili	Grilled Chicken with Roasted Sweet Potatoes and Green Beans	Berry Parfait	Sodium: 909mg Potassium: 2035mg
3	Whole Grain Breakfast Burrito	Mediterranean Tuna Salad	Vegetable Lentil Soup	Mango Coconut Chia Popsicles	Sodium: 1420mg Potassium: 1560mg
4	Yogurt and Berry Smoothie	Oven Fried Chicken	Herbed Butter Pork Chops	Baked Apple Chips	Sodium: 488mg Potassium: 951mg
5	Spinach and Feta Breakfast Wrap	Pork Chops and Apples	Turkey and Vegetable Stir-Fry	Berry Quinoa Parfait	Sodium: 1111mg Potassium: 1735mg
6	Smoked Salmon Breakfast Toast	Tuna Salad Lettuce Wraps	Baked Salmon with Quinoa and Roasted Vegetables	Strawberry Banana Smoothie	Sodium: 1010mg Potassium: 1390mg
	Avocado and Egg Toast	Ground Beef and Bell Peppers	Baked Cod with Lemon-Herb Quinoa	Watermelon Fruit Pizza	Sodium: 796mg Potassium: 2008mg

Week 5

Days	Breakfast	Lunch	Dinner	Dessert	Nutrition
1	Whole Wheat Banana Pancakes	Turkey and Avocado Wrap	Turkey Meatballs with Whole Wheat Pasta	Cinnamon Baked Apples	Sodium: 1160mg Potassium: 1440mg
2	Green Smoothie Bowl	Caprese Salad	Pork with Dates Sauce	Frozen Yogurt Bark	Sodium: 781mg Potassium: 1799mg
3	Overnight Chia Pudding	Greek Quinoa Salad	Lentil and Vegetable Curry	Quinoa Fruit Salad	Sodium: 790mg Potassium: 1330mg
4	Sweet Potato Hash with Eggs	Chicken Chop Suey	Salmon with Quinoa and Steamed Broccoli	Coconut Chia Pudding	Sodium: 670mg Potassium: 2090mg
5	Quinoa Breakfast Bowl	Caprese Pasta Salad	Spiced Up Pork Chops	Greek Yogurt with Honey and Nuts	Sodium: 481mg Potassium: 1352mg
6	Spinach and Feta Omelette	Lentil and Vegetable Soup	Pork and Sweet Potatoes	Cocoa Banana Smoothie Bowl	Sodium: 1169mg Potassium: 2300mg
7	Smashed Avocado Toast	Greek Turkey Burgers	Grilled Veggie and Halloumi Skewers	Peach and Raspberry Crisp	Sodium: 1120mg Potassium: 1480mg

Week 6

Days	Breakfast	Lunch	Dinner	Dessert	Nutrition
1	Cottage Cheese and Fruit Bowl	Pork and Pumpkin Chili	Grilled Chicken with Roasted Sweet Potatoes and Green Beans	Berry Parfait	Sodium: 909mg Potassium: 2035mg
2	Whole Grain Breakfast Burrito	Mediterranean Tuna Salad	Vegetable Lentil Soup	Mango Coconut Chia Popsicles	Sodium: 1420mg Potassium: 1560mg
3	Yogurt and Berry Smoothie	Oven Fried Chicken	Herbed Butter Pork Chops	Baked Apple Chips	Sodium: 488mg Potassium: 951mg
4	Spinach and Feta Breakfast Wrap	Pork Chops and Apples	Turkey and Vegetable Stir-Fry	Berry Quinoa Parfait	Sodium: 1111mg Potassium: 1735mg
5	Smoked Salmon Breakfast Toast	Tuna Salad Lettuce Wraps	Baked Salmon with Quinoa and Roasted Vegetables	Strawberry Banana Smoothie	Sodium: 1010mg Potassium: 1390mg
6	Avocado and Egg Toast	Ground Beef and Bell Peppers	Baked Cod with Lemon-Herb Quinoa	Watermelon Fruit Pizza	Sodium: 796mg Potassium: 2008mg
7	Berry Chia Pudding	Greek Chickpea Salad	Baked Cod with Quinoa and Steamed Asparagus	Chia Seed Pudding	Sodium: 855mg Potassium: 1380mg

Week 7

Days	Breakfast	Lunch	Dinner	Dessert	Nutrition
1	Chia Seed Pudding with Berries	Cajun Pork Chops	Chicken Stir-Fry with Brown Rice	Raspberry Chia Seed Pudding	Sodium: 786mgm Potassium: 1372mg
2	Whole Wheat Banana Pancakes	Turkey and Avocado Wrap	Turkey Meatballs with Whole Wheat Pasta	Cinnamon Baked Apples	Sodium: 1160mg Potassium: 1440mg
3	Green Smoothie Bowl	Caprese Salad	Pork with Dates Sauce	Frozen Yogurt Bark	Sodium: 781mg Potassium: 1799mg
4	Overnight Chia Pudding	Greek Quinoa Salad	Lentil and Vegetable Curry	Quinoa Fruit Salad	Sodium: 790mg Potassium: 1330mg
5	Sweet Potato Hash with Eggs	Chicken Chop Suey	Salmon with Quinoa and Steamed Broccoli	Coconut Chia Pudding	Sodium: 670mg Potassium: 2090mg
6	Quinoa Breakfast Bowl	Caprese Pasta Salad	Spiced Up Pork Chops	Greek Yogurt with Honey and Nuts	Sodium: 481mg Potassium: 1352mg
7	Spinach and Feta Omelette	Lentil and Vegetable Soup	Pork and Sweet Potatoes	Cocoa Banana Smoothie Bowl	Sodium: 1169mg Potassium: 2300mg

Week 8

Days	Breakfast	Lunch	Dinner	Dessert	Nutrition
1	Smashed Avocado Toast	Greek Turkey Burgers	Grilled Veggie and Halloumi Skewers	Peach and Raspberry Crisp	Sodium: 1120mg Potassium: 1480mg
2	Cottage Cheese and Fruit Bowl	Pork and Pumpkin Chili	Grilled Chicken with Roasted Sweet Potatoes and Green Beans	Berry Parfait	Sodium: 909mg Potassium: 2035mg
3	Whole Grain Breakfast Burrito	Mediterranean Tuna Salad	Vegetable Lentil Soup	Mango Coconut Chia Popsicles	Sodium: 1420mg Potassium: 1560mg
4	Yogurt and Berry Smoothie	Oven Fried Chicken	Herbed Butter Pork Chops	Baked Apple Chips	Sodium: 488mg Potassium: 951mg
5	Spinach and Feta Breakfast Wrap	Pork Chops and Apples	Turkey and Vegetable Stir-Fry	Berry Quinoa Parfait	Sodium: 1111mg Potassium: 1735mg
6	Smoked Salmon Breakfast Toast	Tuna Salad Lettuce Wraps	Baked Salmon with Quinoa and Roasted Vegetables	Strawberry Banana Smoothie	Sodium: 1010mg Potassium: 1390mg
	Avocado and Egg Toast	Ground Beef and Bell Peppers	Baked Cod with Lemon-Herb Quinoa	Watermelon Fruit Pizza	Sodium: 796mg Potassium: 2008mg

Week 9

Days	Breakfast	Lunch	Dinner	Dessert	Nutrition
1	Whole Wheat Banana Pancakes	Turkey and Avocado Wrap	Turkey Meatballs with Whole Wheat Pasta	Cinnamon Baked Apples	Sodium: 1160mg Potassium: 1440mg
2	Green Smoothie Bowl	Caprese Salad	Pork with Dates Sauce	Frozen Yogurt Bark	Sodium: 781mg Potassium: 1799mg
3	Overnight Chia Pudding	Greek Quinoa Salad	Lentil and Vegetable Curry	Quinoa Fruit Salad	Sodium: 790mg Potassium: 1330mg
4	Sweet Potato Hash with Eggs	Chicken Chop Suey	Salmon with Quinoa and Steamed Broccoli	Coconut Chia Pudding	Sodium: 670mg Potassium: 2090mg
5	Quinoa Breakfast Bowl	Caprese Pasta Salad	Spiced Up Pork Chops	Greek Yogurt with Honey and Nuts	Sodium: 481mg Potassium: 1352mg
6	Spinach and Feta Omelette	Lentil and Vegetable Soup	Pork and Sweet Potatoes	Cocoa Banana Smoothie Bowl	Sodium: 1169mg Potassium: 2300mg
7	Smashed Avocado Toast	Greek Turkey Burgers	Grilled Veggie and Halloumi Skewers	Peach and Raspberry Crisp	Sodium: 1120mg Potassium: 1480mg

Week 10

Days	Breakfast	Lunch	Dinner	Dessert	Nutrition
1	Cottage Cheese and Fruit Bowl	Pork and Pumpkin Chili	Grilled Chicken with Roasted Sweet Potatoes and Green Beans	Berry Parfait	Sodium: 909mg Potassium: 2035mg
2	Whole Grain Breakfast Burrito	Mediterranean Tuna Salad	Vegetable Lentil Soup	Mango Coconut Chia Popsicles	Sodium: 1420mg Potassium: 1560mg
3	Yogurt and Berry Smoothie	Oven Fried Chicken	Herbed Butter Pork Chops	Baked Apple Chips	Sodium: 488mg Potassium: 951mg
4	Spinach and Feta Breakfast Wrap	Pork Chops and Apples	Turkey and Vegetable Stir-Fry	Berry Quinoa Parfait	Sodium: 1111mg Potassium: 1735mg
5	Smoked Salmon Breakfast Toast	Tuna Salad Lettuce Wraps	Baked Salmon with Quinoa and Roasted Vegetables	Strawberry Banana Smoothie	Sodium: 1010mg Potassium: 1390mg
6	Avocado and Egg Toast	Ground Beef and Bell Peppers	Baked Cod with Lemon-Herb Quinoa	Watermelon Fruit Pizza	Sodium: 796mg Potassium: 2008mg
7	Berry Chia Pudding	Greek Chickpea Salad	Baked Cod with Quinoa and Steamed Asparagus	Chia Seed Pudding	Sodium: 855mg Potassium: 1380mg

Week 11

Days	Breakfast	Lunch	Dinner	Dessert	Nutrition
1	Chia Seed Pudding with Berries	Cajun Pork Chops	Chicken Stir-Fry with Brown Rice	Raspberry Chia Seed Pudding	Sodium: 786mgm Potassium: 1372mg
2	Whole Wheat Banana Pancakes	Turkey and Avocado Wrap	Turkey Meatballs with Whole Wheat Pasta	Cinnamon Baked Apples	Sodium: 1160mg Potassium: 1440mg
3	Green Smoothie Bowl	Caprese Salad	Pork with Dates Sauce	Frozen Yogurt Bark	Sodium: 781mg Potassium: 1799mg
4	Overnight Chia Pudding	Greek Quinoa Salad	Lentil and Vegetable Curry	Quinoa Fruit Salad	Sodium: 790mg Potassium: 1330mg
5	Sweet Potato Hash with Eggs	Chicken Chop Suey	Salmon with Quinoa and Steamed Broccoli	Coconut Chia Pudding	Sodium: 670mg Potassium: 2090mg
6	Quinoa Breakfast Bowl	Caprese Pasta Salad	Spiced Up Pork Chops	Greek Yogurt with Honey and Nuts	Sodium: 481mg Potassium: 1352mg
7	Spinach and Feta Omelette	Lentil and Vegetable Soup	Pork and Sweet Potatoes	Cocoa Banana Smoothie Bowl	Sodium: 1169mg Potassium: 2300mg

Week 12

Days	Breakfast	Lunch	Dinner	Dessert	Nutrition
1	Smashed Avocado Toast	Greek Turkey Burgers	Grilled Veggie and Halloumi Skewers	Peach and Raspberry Crisp	Sodium: 1120mg Potassium: 1480mg
2	Cottage Cheese and Fruit Bowl	Pork and Pumpkin Chili	Grilled Chicken with Roasted Sweet Potatoes and Green Beans	Berry Parfait	Sodium: 909mg Potassium: 2035mg
3	Whole Grain Breakfast Burrito	Mediterranean Tuna Salad	Vegetable Lentil Soup	Mango Coconut Chia Popsicles	Sodium: 1420mg Potassium: 1560mg
4	Yogurt and Berry Smoothie	Oven Fried Chicken	Herbed Butter Pork Chops	Baked Apple Chips	Sodium: 488mg Potassium: 951mg
5	Spinach and Feta Breakfast Wrap	Pork Chops and Apples	Turkey and Vegetable Stir-Fry	Berry Quinoa Parfait	Sodium: 1111mg Potassium: 1735mg
6	Smoked Salmon Breakfast Toast	Tuna Salad Lettuce Wraps	Baked Salmon with Quinoa and Roasted Vegetables	Strawberry Banana Smoothie	Sodium: 1010mg Potassium: 1390mg
	Avocado and Egg Toast	Ground Beef and Bell Peppers	Baked Cod with Lemon-Herb Quinoa	Watermelon Fruit Pizza	Sodium: 796mg Potassium: 2008mg

Conversion Chart

Volume Equivalents (Liquid)

US Standard	US Standard (ounces)	Metric (approximate)
two tbsps	1 fl. oz.	30 milliliter
quarter teacup	2 fl. oz.	60 milliliter
half teacup	4 fl. oz.	120 milliliter
one teacup	8 fl. oz.	240 milliliter
one and half teacups	12 fl. oz.	355 milliliter
two teacups or one pint	16 fl. oz.	475 milliliter
four teacups or one quart	32 fl. oz.	1 Liter
one gallon	128 fl. oz.	4 Liter

Volume Equivalents (Dry)

US Standard	Metric (approximate)
one-eighth	0.5 milliliter
quarter tsp	1 milliliter
half tsp	2 milliliter
three-quarter tsp	4 milliliter
one tsp	5 milliliter
one tbsp	15 milliliter
quarter teacup	59 milliliter
one-third teacup	79 milliliter
half teacup	118 milliliter
two-third teacup	156 milliliter
three-quarter teacup	177 milliliter
one teacup	235 milliliter
two teacups or one pint	475 milliliter
three teacups	700 milliliter
four teacups or one quart	1 Liter

Oven Temperatures

Fahrenheit (F)	Celsius (C) (approximate)
250 deg. F	120 degrees Celsius
300 deg. F	150 degrees Celsius
325 deg. F	165 degrees Celsius
350 deg. F	180 degrees Celsius
375 deg. F	190 degrees Celsius
400 deg. F	200 degrees Celsius
425 deg. F	220 degrees Celsius
450 deg. F	230 degrees Celsius

Weight Equivalents

US Standard	Metric (approximate)
one tbsp	15 gm
half oz.	15 gm
one oz.	30 gm
two oz.	60 gm
four oz.	115 gm
eight oz.	225 gm
twelve oz.	340 gm
sixteen oz or one lb.	455 gm

Index

Avocado and Egg Toast; 20
Avocado Hummus; 38
Baked Apple Chips; 54
Baked Chicken Breast with Roasted Vegetables; 64
Baked Cod with Herbed Crust; 62
Baked Cod with Lemon-Herb Quinoa; 31
Baked Cod with Quinoa and Steamed Asparagus; 34
Baked Potato; 81
Baked Salmon with Asparagus; 63
Baked Salmon with Quinoa and Roasted Vegetables; 32
Beetroot Carrot Juice; 58
Berry Blast Smoothie; 56
Berry Chia Pudding; 21
Berry Parfait; 51
Berry Quinoa Parfait; 53
Blueberry Almond Smoothie; 59
Blueberry Spinach Smoothie; 57
Broccoli and Bean Casserole; 76
Brown Rice Pilaf with Vegetables; 44
Cajun Pork Chops; 28
Caprese Pasta Salad; 24
Caprese Salad; 23
Caprese Skewers; 40
Caprese Skewers with Balsamic Glaze; 44
Caramelized Pork Chops; 63
Cauliflower and Potato Curry; 72
Chia Seed Pudding; 50
Chia Seed Pudding with Berries; 19
Chicken Chili; 61
Chicken Chop Suey; 23
Chicken Stir-Fry with Brown Rice; 35
Chickpea and Vegetable Curry; 70
Chickpea and Vegetable Stew; 69
Cinnamon Baked Apples; 52
Cocoa Banana Smoothie Bowl; 52
Coconut Chia Pudding; 50
Cottage Cheese and Fruit Bowl; 19
Cucumber and Hummus Roll-Ups; 39
Cucumber and Tomato Salad; 45
Cucumber and Watermelon Salad; 46
Eggplant Parmesan; 65
Frozen Yogurt Bark; 52
Ginger and Chili Baked Fish; 78

Greek Chickpea Salad; 27
Greek Cucumber Cups; 41
Greek Quinoa Salad; 26
Greek Salad; 73
Greek Salad Skewers; 39
Greek Turkey Burgers; 27
Greek Yogurt and Fruit Parfait; 42
Greek Yogurt Parfait; 66
Greek Yogurt with Honey and Nuts; 53
Green Detox Juice; 58
Green Smoothie Bowl; 18
Grilled Chicken with Roasted Sweet Potatoes and Green Beans; 34
Grilled Eggplant with Balsamic Glaze; 48
Grilled Pineapple with Yogurt and Honey; 77
Grilled Salmon with Papaya-Mint Salsa; 81
Grilled Vegetable Pasta; 76
Grilled Vegetable Skewers with Tofu; 82
Grilled Veggie and Halloumi Skewers; 30
Ground Beef and Bell Peppers; 25
Healthy Vegetable Fried Rice; 71
Herbed Butter Pork Chops; 35
Kiwi Spinach Smoothie; 56
Lemon Garlic Roasted Zucchini; 47
Lemon Herb Roasted Turkey Breast; 81
Lentil and Vegetable Curry; 34
Lentil and Vegetable Soup; 24
Lentil and Vegetable Stir-Fried Rice; 73
Lentil Soup; 66
Mango Basil Smoothie; 56
Mango Coconut Chia Popsicles; 53
Mango Salsa; 40
Mango Turmeric Smoothie; 59
Matcha Green Tea Latte; 56
Mediterranean Chicken Skewers; 76
Mediterranean Chickpea Salad; 73
Mediterranean Pasta Salad; 64
Mediterranean Pork; 62
Mediterranean Quinoa Bowl; 69
Mediterranean Tuna Salad; 26
Mussels with Creamy Tarragon Sauce; 78
Orange Carrot Ginger Juice; 57
Oven Fried Chicken; 27
Oven-Baked Zucchini Chips; 41
Oven-Roasted Green Beans; 47

Overnight Chia Pudding; 17

Peach and Raspberry Crisp; 51

Pineapple Coconut Smoothie; 57

Pineapple Ginger Turmeric Smoothie; 59

Pomegranate Mint Cooler; 57

Pork and Pumpkin Chili; 23

Pork and Sweet Potatoes; 33

Pork Chops and Apples; 25

Pork with Dates Sauce; 33

Pressure Cooker Lentil Sloppy Joes with Coleslaw; 79

Quinoa and Black Bean Salad Cups; 41

Quinoa and Vegetable Salad; 45

Quinoa and Vegetable Stir-Fry; 68

Quinoa Breakfast Bowl; 19

Quinoa Fruit Salad; 50

Quinoa Salad Cups; 38

Quinoa Stuffed Bell Peppers; 65

Raspberry Chia Seed Pudding; 51

Raspberry Lime Spritzer; 58

Ratatouille; 69

Roasted Beet and Arugula Salad; 46

Roasted Brussels Sprouts with Balsamic Glaze; 47

Roasted Red Pepper Hummus; 40

Salmon with Quinoa and Steamed Broccoli; 32

Sesame Salmon with Broccoli and Tomatoes; 77

Smashed Avocado Toast; 21

Smashed Chickpea Salad Wraps; 38

Smoked Salmon Breakfast Toast; 20

Sparkling Lemonade; 57

Spiced Up Pork Chops; 31

Spinach and Feta Breakfast Wrap; 21

Spinach and Feta Omelette; 20

Spinach and Mushroom Omelette; 61

Spinach and Mushroom Quiche; 45

Spinach Falafel Wrap; 79

Steamed Asparagus with Lemon Butter Sauce; 46

Steamed Asparagus with Lemon Garlic Sauce; 44

Steamed Broccoli with Lemon Garlic Sauce; 47

Steamed Edamame with Sea Salt; 48

Strawberry Banana Smoothie; 50

Summer Vegetable Sauté; 68

Swedish Spicy Carrot with Cod; 80

Sweet Potato and Black Bean Chili; 68

Sweet Potato Hash with Eggs; 18

Taco-Seasoned Roast Beef Wraps; 77

Tuna Cucumber Bites; 39

Tuna Salad Lettuce Wraps; 26

Tuna Stuffed Cucumber Bites; 38

Turkey and Avocado Wrap; 25

Turkey and Vegetable Skewers; 61

Turkey and Vegetable Stir-Fry; 33

Turkey Meatballs with Marinara Sauce; 63

Turkey Meatballs with Whole Wheat Pasta; 30

Vegetable and Lentil Curry; 72

Vegetable Lentil Soup; 31

Veggie and Brown Rice Stir-Fry; 71

Veggie Lentil Burgers; 70

Veggie Quesadillas; 64

Watermelon Fruit Pizza; 52

Whole Grain Breakfast Burrito; 17

Whole Wheat Banana Pancakes; 18

Yogurt and Berry Smoothie; 17

Yogurt-Dipped Strawberries; 42

Conclusion

The DASH diet, which stands for "Dietary Approaches to Stop Hypertension," is a unique approach to address one of the leading causes of death in the 21st century—high blood pressure. With one in three adults affected by hypertension, the DASH diet focuses on promoting a healthy lifestyle to combat this condition. By following this diet, individuals can lower their blood pressure, reduce the risk of associated diseases like heart problems, kidney issues, and diabetes, and achieve sustainable weight loss.

The DASH diet sets itself apart from other diets by emphasizing lower sodium levels and higher intakes of potassium, calcium, fiber, and magnesium. This approach supports overall blood pressure reduction without harming the body's natural processes. Notably, the diet has proven effective in eliminating hypertension-related disorders like osteoporosis, diabetes, and kidney failure.

Originally developed to lower blood pressure naturally, the DASH diet gained recognition from the US National Institute of Health and has been endorsed by reputable organizations such as the American Heart Association. It is not exclusively for individuals with hypertension but can be followed by anyone seeking improved health and scientific weight loss. The diet's success lies in providing essential nutrients, controlling sodium intake, and keeping individuals satisfied without causing metabolic disruptions.

While weight loss was initially not the primary focus of the DASH diet, further research led to the inclusion of a systematic weight loss plan. By incorporating nutritious foods like nuts, whole fruits and vegetables, and whole grains, the diet helps individuals manage their weight effectively. Unlike unreliable fad diets, the DASH diet is based on scientific principles and offers personalized plans tailored to individual needs.

The DASH diet has been refined over time to optimize health and reduce hypertension by increasing protein intake and reducing unhealthy fats and empty carbs. This evidence-based approach supports sustainable weight loss while maintaining a healthy metabolism. By following the DASH diet, individuals can regulate blood sugar levels, decrease triglycerides, lower LDL cholesterol, improve HDL cholesterol, and experience an overall improvement in well-being.

Even if individuals do not have hypertension, they can adopt the DASH diet to promote internal health. Incorporating the diet gradually rather than making sudden changes is advised to ensure a comfortable transition. It is possible that individuals are already consuming foods aligned with the DASH diet without realizing it. Making a list of compatible items and considering healthy choices while dining out can further support adherence to the diet.

The DASH diet offers a scientifically supported approach to lowering blood pressure, preventing associated diseases, and achieving sustainable weight loss. By emphasizing nutritious foods and personalized plans, this diet can benefit anyone seeking improved health and well-being.

Made in the USA
Las Vegas, NV
22 December 2023

83435911R00057